John Milton

Blackwell Introductions to Literature

This series sets out to provide concise and stimulating introductions to literary subjects. It offers books on major authors (from William Shakespeare to James Joyce), as well as key periods and movements (from Anglo-Saxon literature to the contemporary). Coverage is also afforded to such specific topics as 'Arthurian Romance'. While some of the volumes are classed as 'short introductions' (under 200 pages), others are slightly longer books (around 250 pages). All are written by outstanding scholars as texts to inspire newcomers and others: nonspecialists wishing to revisit a topic, or general readers. The prospective overall aim is to ground and prepare students and readers of whatever kind in their pursuit of wider reading.

John Milton
A Short Introduction

Roy Flannagan

Blackwell Publishers

Editorial Offices:
108 Cowley Road, Oxford OX4 1JF, UK
  Tel: +44 (0)1865 791100
350 Main Street, Malden, MA 02148-5018, USA
  Tel: +1 781 388 8250

First published 2002 by Blackwell Publishers Ltd, a Blackwell Publishing company

Library of Congress Cataloging-in-Publication Data

Flannagan, Roy
    John Milton — a short introduction / Roy Flannagan
        p.   cm. — (Blackwell introductions to literature)
    Includes bibliographical references and index.
    ISBN 0–631–22619–2 (alk. paper) — ISBN 0–631–22620–6 (pb.:alk.paper)
    1. Milton, John, 1608–1674 — Criticism and interpretation.   I. Title.
    II. Series.

    PR3588 .F585 2002
    821'.4—dc21

                                                                2001003942

A catalogue record for this title is available from the British Library.

Set in 10.5 on 13 pt Meridien
by Ace Filmsetting Ltd, Frome, Somerset
Printed in Great Britain by TJ International, Padstow, Cornwall

For further information on
Blackwell Publishers, visit our website:
www.blackwellpublishers.co.uk

Contents

Illustrations

Preface

I should say what this little book is not. It is not a handbook to Milton, nor is it a series of plot-summaries of the major works. It assumes that its reader is falling in love with Milton's poetry, or has already, and that the reader wants to know more about what people think about the poetry, the man, the historical context. A reader might also want to know what makes Milton great. This was my own first reaction to the power of his poetry, as a graduate student. I was moved and excited, but I wanted to know why and how the poetry and then the prose excited me. I wanted to know what sort of person Milton was, I wanted to know his relationship with other great poets and dramatists writing before him, I wanted to know what he was like to his own family and friends. I wanted to know what made him a genius, what made him an artist for all time.

In writing this book, after living with Milton, so to speak, for over 30 years, I challenged myself to examine new ideas or ideas that were still evolving in my own mind, based on the especially huge amount of criticism published since the early sixties that I had witnessed firsthand as editor of the *Milton Quarterly*. Though I was brought up feeling the influence of New Critics and descriptive bibliographers, I have felt the strength of feminist, structuralist, semiotic, new-historicist, reader-response, eco-critical and other valuable schools, but I very much wanted to avoid the cant of any currently popular school. I wanted to talk to readers very much as I might talk to a class of excited undergraduates, or to someone I had just met in an airport, sharing their enthusiasm, not talking down to them and not trying to impress them with how much I knew. I wanted to give that kind of audience a good read. I would like to help any new reader of Milton who would like to know more about him, or to help show a reader returning to Milton how good a writer he is. I did not want to impress anyone with how smart Milton was, or with how much I have read about him. I have kept the scholarship quiet, and left the reader to find other major reference works.

To that end, I have organized this book to be read rather than consulted. I asked bright friends and fellow enthusiasts like Ann Gulden and Angelica Duran to read drafts of what I was writing in earlier stages, and I asked them to mark what I had written that they hadn't thought about yet – anything that seemed to be a new idea. Then I went back in and worked on what seemed the freshest points. My editor at Blackwell, Andrew McNeillie, has been very supportive of the project from its inception, and has given me only the best of tips about how to translate American colloquialism into English understanding; and my longtime friend and fellow monk to Milton, Gordon Campbell, has helped me keep my biographical and critical points as accurate as I can.

The organization of the book is chronological, and it mixes biography with literary criticism, but I have tried to allow it to grow organically from major points rather than be dominated by chronological or spatial coherence. The headings along the way, the signposts, are there only to tell the reader that I am changing direction slightly, or to tease the reader to think of something new. At times I meant to be provoking or provocative, teasing but not bullying the reader into an unusual position. I believe in keeping an open mind for myself and for the reader about one of the clearest, yet most enigmatic and even mysterious, of great writers. I also see Milton as having a keen sense of humor which sometimes can laugh sardonically at his struggling reader, so I approach him with humor and with the sense that reading him can be a good time for the companionable reader. I enjoy being around Milton and laughing with him as he laughs at my limitations.

R. F.
September 2001.

The Family Background

The poet John Milton was born on December 9, 1608, into a prosperous bourgeois family. His father, John Sr., leased a large portion of a handsome store-front on Bread Street, at best a five-minute walk from the spiritual and mercantile center of London, St. Paul's Cathedral. The Gothic St. Paul's (not the building designed by Christopher Wren that stands now but the old St. Paul's, which was destroyed in the Great Fire) had a number of stalls for bookselling in its famous churchyard, and exterior alcoves where youthful choirboys performed plays written by Shakespeare's great rival dramatists such as John Marston – the same performers, perhaps, that Hamlet complained about as competitors to his players, "little eyeasses" (the unfledged hawks of *Hamlet* II.viii.339). According to John Stow's *Survey of London*, Bread Street "is now [1603] wholly inhabited by rich merchants; and divers fair inns be there, for good receipt of carriers and other travellers to the city" (309). On Bread Street, originally named for the commodity sold there, the Milton house was given the name "The Black Spread Eagle" – which was to become the Milton coat of arms and would be used by John Milton the poet to seal official or legal documents (plate 1).

The house was not far from the Boar's Head Tavern and the Mermaid Tavern (both downhill from the Milton's house and closer to the Fleet and the Thames rivers), and a few blocks from the Blackfriars Theater, a Shakespearean enterprise in which John Milton Sr. was a shareholder. Milton mentions both Jonson and Shakespeare – frequenters of the Boar's Head and the Mermaid – with some knowledge and some affection in his early poetry.

John Milton Sr. was a scrivener – a professional draftsman and a combination of lawyer, moneylender before banks came into existence, and real-estate agent. Scriveners were thought to be allied with the devil by those who envied their prosperity, because they were considered crafty businessmen who made money too rapidly (Beal 195). Milton Sr. must have been unusual even in his own time, because he was not only a prosperous burgher but a composer

Plate 1   Milton's personal seal, based on the spread-eagle sign of his father's shop. From S. L. Sotheby, *Ramblings in the Elucidation of the Autograph of Milton* (London: Thomas Richards, 1861). © British Library, London.

of music respectable enough to be played for Queen Elizabeth. As a scrivener, he loaned money to aristocrats such as Sir Fulke Greville or Sir Francis Leigh, nephew of John Egerton, Earl of Bridgewater, who would become his son's patron for the masque performed in Ludlow (Campbell, *Chronology* 23–4).

The Milton family was from Oxfordshire, of yeoman stock, landholders but not members of the aristocracy. Richard Milton, the poet's grandfather, was an intolerant Roman Catholic who was supposed to have ejected his son John from his household for reading in an English Bible. The elder John was said to have attended Christ Church, the Oxford college, and he may have received musical training there. The poet never mentioned his grandfather, but his family's continued business dealings in Oxfordshire would lead him to his first wife, Mary Powell, whose family lived not far from the Milton house.

The neighborhood the Miltons lived in in London was full of wealthy tradesmen and public officials – drapers, salt merchants, goldsmiths, merchant tailors, aldermen, sheriffs, even Lord Mayors of London. It was a proud but decidedly unaristocratic neighborhood, and Milton would never leave his bourgeois London setting for long. His father's house, or his part of the corporate tenement or condo-

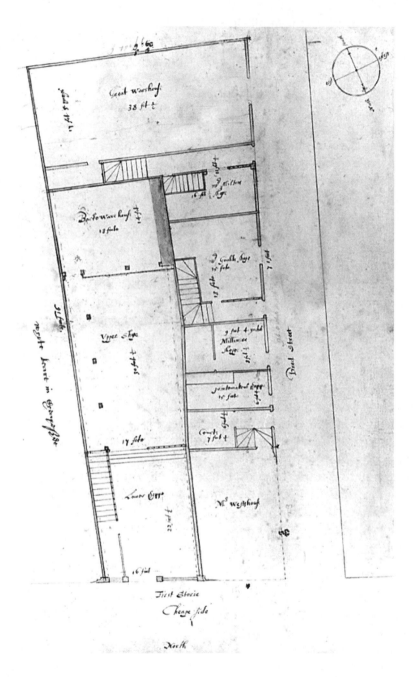

Plate 2   The White Bear, Cheapside: ground-floor plan. By permission of Eton College Archives.

minium in which the family lived, included four stories above ground level, with "Mr Miltons shope" on ground level and "Mr Milton's Hall" up above, with kitchen and bedrooms leading on up to another set of rooms and then a garret four floors off the ground (plate 2; Blakiston) filled with trade shops of a "Milliner or Leather Seller" (haberdasher, seller of hats and other "pretty toies for Gentle women" [*OED* sense 2.b, citing Thomas Nashe, 1592]), a "Poynte maker" (lace-worker or maker of laces), a girdler (maker of belts to hold purses or swords), a grocer, Milton's dad's "scrivener Shopp under the kitchen," a shop owned by the Merchant Taylors (the guild or union of tailors who supplied their own cloth, founders of a famous school in London and others elsewhere), a counting house (book-keeping office), a buttery (storage room for foodstuffs, ale, bread, and butter). I assume that the large house was called "the White Beare" because it had once been a public house. So Milton Jr. lived over his father's shop, and the family could buy groceries, leather goods, or hats on site, or have a suit made at the shop owned by the Merchant Taylors' company. The house located the scrivener's shop near the busy intersection of Cheapside and Bread Street, with five doorways facing Bread Street for easy access to the various business offices or shops.

The near presence of the great church of St. Paul; the bustling trade of books, food, and nonperishable goods; and the politics of Queen Elizabeth's and King James's realm focused in nearby Westminster: all these activities would have stirred the mind of the younger John Milton, who was born five years after Elizabeth died, into a period of peace, prosperity, and mercantile and cultural exchange. The City was proud of its trade, and tradesmen were on the rise toward the respectable status of noblemen. John Milton Sr. made loans to titled gentlemen, and John Jr. would be privately educated by tutors, sent to what was perhaps the best preparatory school in London, and he would be allowed to finish his education at Christ's College, Cambridge. Still, his father made money by lending it, and the family was "in trade," gaining respectability only by having money and spending it on education. Tradesmen were not permitted to wear silk in public, according to the sumptuary laws no longer enforced during Milton's youth.

The sign of bourgeois pride on John Milton the Scrivener's front door – the double eagle of the scrivener's trade – would inevitably become his son's coat of arms, as John Milton Jr. traveled to respectability by attending the cathedral school of St. Paul's (where he was a pigeon, not an eagle) and then graduating from Christ's College. By the time he reached adulthood, Milton's circle of friends and pupils was to include Katherine Jones, Viscountess Ranelagh; her nephew Richard Berry, second Earl of Barrymore; Lady Margaret Lee; Lord Carberry; and he may even have met several Church of England bishops that he saw fit to memorialize after their deaths. There is no evidence that Milton was ever scorned in his relations with aristocrats known to him because of class differences. Nor did he have to seek patronage by groveling. He was obviously comfortable with tailors and booksellers, with well-read Quakers, with the headmaster of Eton College, and perhaps only slightly less so with lords and ladies.

Milton's Education

The child John Milton, first-born son of John the Scrivener, seems to have been his father's favorite, as evidenced by the son's respectful and loving tribute in the Latin elegy *"Ad Patrem"* ("To My Father," possibly written in 1638). Christopher Milton, the poet's brother, did lead a distinguished life as a Cambridge-educated lawyer and later a Member of Parliament for Reading.

From a very early age the child John Milton must have been cherished by his family as something of an educational phenomenon, given to reading, translating, and writing. His father provided tutors in various subjects, and even paid a maidservant to be sure that tapers were lit during late nights when the child John wanted to read. Though very little is known about Milton's mother Sara, her son describes her as charitable and good-hearted, almost saintly, and she would be buried in the nave of the parish church at Horton, a place of honor and dignity. The home atmosphere in the house on Bread Street must have nurtured and perhaps indulged the prodigy. There is even some evidence that Milton may have been sent out of London for part of his private schooling.

St. Paul's School, which occupied a handsome neoclassical building adjacent to the cathedral, was noted for its founder, the humanist John Colet; and it was also known for its choirboys, sometimes called "Paul's Pigeons," the idea being that they flocked around the cathedral like the ever-present cathedral birds. In the 1590s and early 1600s St. Paul's was also celebrated for its acting troupe, similar to those troupes of boy-actors that Hamlet complains about as rivals to the kind of companies of mature men in which Shakespeare himself performed.

The school had a rigorous classical curriculum, and it provided thorough grounding in the principal languages of the Christian Bible, Latin and Greek, with perhaps a smattering of Hebrew, if one could find a tutor who could teach it. In the halls of the school, only Latin was spoken. Milton's early school training would have covered authors like Ovid, Cicero, Vergil, and Julius Caesar – much as would Shakespeare's training at a grammar school in Stratford. By any reckoning, though, Milton was much more thoroughly educated than Shakespeare, if not as deeply schooled in London street-life or the life of a Stratford magistrate or bumpkin.

Milton bonded with Alexander Gil, the son of the headmaster of the same name at St. Paul's School and himself a teacher there, and the two exchanged letters and poetry for some years after Milton graduated. Gil the younger may have contributed to Milton's – at the time – radical politics, to which another of Milton's tutors, Thomas Young, may also have introduced his pupil. One of Milton's schoolmasters, we are told by John Aubrey, had the boy cut his hair short, in the manner of the Puritans (so labeled because they were trying to restore the English church to what they considered to be the primitive purity and simplicity of the very early Christian church). We have a portrait which is very apt to be the boy Milton, well-dressed but with very short hair, no doubt commissioned, probably by a continental portraitist, Cornelius Janson (or Janssen), by his proud parents.

Though Puritan sects grew in number and influence during the late years of Queen Elizabeth and the early years of King James, the larger and more obvious enemy of the English church was the religion of Milton's grandfather, Roman Catholicism, reviled in England as the Whore of Babylon or Seven-Headed Beast (Rome with its seven hills) or, more simply, as Papism or what Protestants thought to be misapplied worship of the Pope or of Rome. A Roman Catholic conspiracy attempted to blow up King James and the Houses of Parliament on November 5, 1605 – the Gunpowder Plot now celebrated on Guy Fawkes Day. The youthful Milton wrote several Latin poems to celebrate the escape of the English church from Roman oppression and the English monarch from annihilation.

Milton may have had a love–hate relationship with Roman Catholics, perhaps because his grandfather was one. He could say, after his trip to continental Europe in 1638 and 1639, that some of his best friends were Italian Roman Catholics, but we know he would anger some of them with his own Protestantism, while he was in Italy and after he had returned to England. Even in his letters to Roman Catholic friends in Italy, Milton could be abrasive about a religion he thought to be more Satanic than godly, and one of the only bits of obvious satire in *Paradise Lost* is devoted to a Limbo or Paradise of Fools (3.495), where foolish monks roll and writhe for an eternity, circled superstitiously by their cowls and beads.

Milton's relationship with his father remained positive and unabrasive throughout their years together. The father must have financed his son's travels in Europe, with a manservant to accompany him at one point and a hired hermit guide at another, and Milton Senior provided his son with what that son called "studious retirement" at family dwellings in Hammersmith (from about 1632), west of London and near to it, and at Horton (by 1637; now in Berkshire, but until 1974 in Buckinghamshire [see Campbell 64]). Milton the son was not on his own and out of his father's household until after his return from mainland Europe, in 1640, when he took lodgings in London and accepted pupils in a day-school, beginning with his own nephews, Edward and John Phillips. Reciprocally, Milton would take in his father to live with his family, when his father was old and infirm. Throughout his life, Milton Junior benefitted from his father's investments deeded to him. Neither father nor son hesitated to sue deadbeat clients or tenants, to protect their investments or to collect their rents.

At Christ's, the Cambridge college, in 1627, Milton, being proud, gifted, opinionated, and perhaps spoiled enough to engage in an educational agenda of his own making, disagreed with his first tutor, William Chappell, and he was "rusticated," sent back home from the University, as a result. He may even have been whipped by Chappell (Aubrey in *Riverside* 4 has "whipped him" curiously in the margin of his notes about Milton's biography), and he held a grudge against his uncongenial tutor the rest of his life. When Milton returned to Christ's College, he would be placed under the tutelage of Nathaniel Tovey, whose opinions were apparently much better fitted to the poet's educational and religious leanings than were Chappell's (when Christopher Milton came to Cambridge, Tovey became his tutor as well, indicating that the family still approved of Tovey).

Milton's college career seems to have been divided between a stage of mutual hostility between his classmates and the arrogant and brilliant young poet – perhaps the first several years of his college career – and a stage of mutual respect, during which the eccentric and fastidious but elegant young poet John Milton was gradually accepted by his college peers, just as a modern computer nerd or intellectual might gradually be accepted by schoolmates because of obvious intelligence. Milton's college nickname, "the Lady of Christ's," seems to be a label that may have called attention to his pale complexion, his beauty, and his delicate or fastidious manners. After a few years of living with the nickname, Milton could accept the label and joke about it. One index to Milton's progress toward likeableness among his college mates is the use of jokes in his prolusions (formal and informal assigned school orations). He is capable of picturing dissolute Cambridge students as ridiculously macho drinkers and self-loving foolish prancers, and he compares them with Shakespeare's Trinculo in *The Tempest* (see *An Apology*, *Yale* 1.887); but in the latter part of Milton's college career he jokes with his fellow students convivially. In his later prolusions, Milton makes fun of the names of some of his classmates more gently and unmaliciously, as with Latin puns on the English name "Rivers." If he was the lady, they were the muddy waters.

Milton and Shakespeare

When biographers and critics use the word " puritan" of Milton, the word has a context from the religious upheavals of the seventeenth century, not quite our modern meaning. Milton used the term to refer to a religious party out of favor with the king, but he also understood that the Protestant reformers of his own time were branded with the name "Puritans" (*Columbia* 5.45), and he understood that people labeled "puritan" might be driven to America by the prelates (*Columbia* 3.50).

John Milton is not Shakespeare's Malvolio, the sour and hypocritical puritan, saying "Thou shalt not" to anyone who dared to enjoy cakes and ale. The young Milton led a full life, attending plays, playing music with his own portable organ or stringed instruments like the viol, reading good books, sitting for a portrait by a respectable continental artist, watching girls in London parks. When he was in Italy, in 1638, Milton admitted that he was driven into a kind of ecstasy by listening to a popular operatic singer, Leonora Baroni, and he wrote poems in Latin celebrating the artistic and the sensual power of her voice.

Milton did have the good poetic taste to celebrate the man he called "sweetest *Shakespeare*" and, possessively, "my *Shakespeare*," in his own early poetry. Like Shakespeare, Milton would write exquisite lyrics (songs to be set to music), respectable sonnets, and several dramatic entertainments not unlike Shakespeare's *Midsummer Night's Dream* or *The Tempest* in spirit, theme, or execution. We know now that John Milton Sr. was a shareholder in one of Shakespeare's theaters, the Blackfriars, and that Milton may have borrowed phrases for his own memorial poem to Shakespeare from one of Shakespeare's unpublished poems in memory of a theatrical patron (Campbell, "Shakespeare").

Milton had an unusually sure sense of what great poetry was: at one time or another, in his poetry and prose, he declared his kinship to Shakespeare, Ben Jonson, Edmund Spenser, and Sir Philip Sidney, with Chaucer and John Gower providing earlier English poetic inspiration, as they did for Shakespeare. Through St. Paul's Cathedral, Milton must also have come into contact with John Donne as preacher, but Milton might not have known of Donne's poetry, even if what we now call the metaphysical style, with its extremely esoteric and intellectual imagery, might have influenced some of his youthful English poetry. Milton never took seriously a poetic style that emphasized startling or grotesque imagery.

Of course, Milton need not have written his own poetry exclusively in English: he could just as easily have written in the universal language of poetry and prose, Latin, and he also wrote poetry – and not bad poetry – in Italian.

Like Shakespeare but of the very next generation, Milton was a child of the Protestant Reformation; his family was split by the same forces that Shakespeare made fun of in *Twelfth Night*, including Malvolio's sour variety of puritanism. John Milton's Roman Catholic grandfather threw his father out of his house simply because "he found a Bible in English in his chamber" (Aubrey in *Riverside* 2). Shakespeare, as a sometime Roman Catholic sympathizer (why else have a ghost in Purgatory?) must have known the same sort of intolerance within his own family.

The omnivorous reader

Despite the fact that there are some very well-read scholars now studying Milton, and some of those have considerable linguistic abilities, reading at least four or five languages easily, there is no one that I know of, living or dead, who has read all the books that we know Milton read in his lifetime. The man was a phenomenal linguist, comfortable in French, Italian, Spanish, Latin, Greek, at least knowledgeable about Hebrew, Arabic, Syriac, Aramaic, and what was known as Chaldaic. He tried his hand at understanding Chaucer, certainly, and he may have deciphered elements of Anglo-Saxon on his own. He compiled manuscript dictionaries in Latin and Greek, dictionaries so precise and complete that they were used as models for later printed dictionaries. He helped provide paper for and he may have contributed to Brian Walton's *Polyglot Bible* of the early 1650s, an amazing printing feat for its time, with the Old Testament texts spread out in its various languages across double pages. He compiled a theological index, apparently, based on his extensive readings in biblical commentary and his study of the early Church Fathers, who wrote in Latin and Greek.

Milton kept what was called a commonplace book, notes and citations for his own use organized under headings of topics he was interested in, such as kingship or polygamy. Just how extensive his reading is can be deduced for entries he made from about 1644 to 1650 (Campbell 79):

Johanes Leunclavius, *Juris Graeco-Romani*
John Selden, *Uxor Hebraica*
Sigismund von Herberstein, *Rerum Moscoviticarum Commentarii*
Alessandro Tassoni, *Pensieri*
Trajano Boccalini, *De' Ragguagli di Parnasso*
Jacob Philipp Tomasini, *Petrarcha Redivivus*
Francesco Berni, *Orlando Innamorato Rifatto*
Wilhelm Schickhard, *Jus Regium Hebraeorum*
Sir Henry Spelman, *Concilia, Decreta, Leges*

Sir Philip Sidney, *Arcadia*
John Guillim, *A Display of Heraldry*
Robert Ward, *Animadversions of Warre, or a Military Magazine of Rules and Instructions for the Managing of Warre*
Theodoret, *Historia Ecclesiastica*
Basil, *Homiliae: In Psalmum I; In Hexameron VIII, In Principium Proverborum*
Crysostom, *In Genesim Homiliae*
Socrates Scholasticus, *Historia Ecclesiastic*
Gregory of Nyssa, *De Virginitate*
Guicciardini, *Historia d'Italia*
Tasso, *Gerusalemme Liberata*
Giovanni Villani, *Croniche Fiorentine*
Codinus, *De Officiis Magnae Ecclesiae et Aulae Constaninopolitanae*
Frontinus, *Strategmata*
Rivetus, *Praelectiones in Exodi*

The range of this short catalogue, based on entries in Milton's commonplace book (which was a kind of intellectual diary based on notes from reading) is amazing for any time. Milton is reading deeply, in the original languages, in Church Fathers and biblical commentary (Gregory, Crysostom, Basil, Rivetus), but at the same time he is investigating military strategy (as with Ward). He is reading books on topics that interest him, as with Gregory of Nyssa on virginity (a subject which his own masque had focused on), the medieval Italian love poet Petrarch, and marriage customs amongst the Jews (Selden). He is reading in ancient law (Leunclavius, Schickhard) but also in poetic theory (Tassoni). He is reading original works and even revisions of the works of Italian epic poets (Tasso, Tassoni, Berni) and he is reading in British and Italian history (Gildas, Guicciardini, Villani), and in ancient Christian church history (Socrates Scholasticus). His reading would require a command of Greek, Latin, French, Hebrew, and Italian, and it would demand thorough knowledge of the cultural history of all of western Europe, including Russia (von Herberstein). No modern scholar, indeed no scholar that I know of from any time after Milton, would have the combined linguistic skills and historical scope to be able to read and comprehend all of what Milton seems to have studied with pleasure and understanding. His reading list also reflects his independence and his political uniqueness: he was all countries and all civilization in one being.

Political Milton

John Milton Jr. would have started a fight with his own brother, the Royalist Christopher Milton, when the poet John took the side of the Parliamentary forces during the English Civil Wars. At times during the various outbreaks of civil war, John Sr. lived with the son who defended the king, Christopher, and at times with the Parliamentary son John. John Milton the poet married Mary, the daughter of a Royalist and Roman Catholic country squire, Richard Powell of Oxfordshire – setting himself up for political and religious household turmoil – and she left him soon after they were married, only to be reunited with him as war raged and the Royalist forces seemed to be losing ground.

Though Milton remained friends with his composer friend Henry Lawes long after they had each declared for an opposite faction, Lawes's Royalism would probably mean that they could not talk about politics when meeting socially. Henry's brother William, also a composer, would die fighting for King Charles I. But in the height of controversy over divorce, bishops, and kingly authority, in 1646, Milton wrote his Sonnet 13, "To Mr Henry Lawes." Conflicts created by religious and civil wars often split husband and wife or brother and brother or friend and friend, as it would split Milton from his family, his friends, or his in-laws.

Critics and biographers still argue over Milton's place in the history of his own time or in the history of ideas. He was undeniably a functionary, a minor player in the government of Oliver Cromwell – unmentioned by Cromwell himself in any recorded conversation or bit of Cromwell's writing, even though Milton served as Latin Secretary or Secretary for Foreign Tongues for the Interregnum government. Milton served as a diplomatic correspondent, as a translator, as a propagandist, as something of a censor of subversive documents, and occasionally as a spy-catcher. In official meetings he stood, while other more important men sat. When his poor eyesight degenerated into blindness during his tenure as a Parliamentary public servant, he was given less and less responsibility. But he was as important as any good propagandist or public- relations person might be, a spin-doctor of the English Civil Wars. He was the spokesperson of his political party, which was the ruling party, in the late 1640s and early 1650s, and he continued to defend what he and others called the "good old cause" (*Yale* 7.462), something a modern reader might identify with government by parliament, even after the Restoration of the monarchy in 1660.

In the area of international relations, he was responsible for correspondence with Queen Christina of Sweden – we know she respected him as a scholar – and he drafted letters to the court of Louis XIV and to Cardinal Mazarin. Even the fact that some of his regicidal books were burned in continental Europe attests to his international notoriety: the kinder phrase he himself used was that "all Europe talks from side to side" (Sonnet 22) about some of his books.

Because of the undying fame of his poetry, and because of the independent fame of *Areopagitica* and the rising reputation of Milton's divorce tracts, he is more famous now in cultural history or history of ideas, or obviously in literary history, than he was in his own time, politically or culturally. Milton's poetic fame, of course, has always boosted the importance of his prose, but his prose tracts have an independent vitality and intellectual force, engaging legal experts, cultural historians, critics emphasizing gender research. He was always controversial in his own time, and he bravely defended his own independence and his own conscience, time after time and sometimes savagely, throughout his public career.

Modern critics and biographers tend to see Milton as prophet rather than just as controversialist. It is true that his views on the separation of church and state, on the comparative liberty of the press from prepublication censorship, and on the freedom within the institution of marriage to declare a divorce on the grounds of incompatibility or cruelty, as well as on the freedom of any people from a monarch who turns tyrant – all of those positions have been adopted by most modern western nations. Most of Milton's dreams of liberty have come true, especially in western, democratic societies.

The prodigy poet

Milton knew from a very early age what his vocation was to be. John Aubrey reports that Milton "was . . . a poet" by 1619, when he was 10 (*Riverside* 2). Some evidence of his early talent is his paraphrase of Psalm 114 and translation of Psalm 135, supposedly "don[e] by the Author at fifteen years old" (*Riverside* 48), influenced by the florid and colorful poetic style of Joshua Sylvester's translation of

DuBartas's *Divine Weekes and Workes*. The young Milton was probably also writing poetry in Latin by the time he was 15, while he was still enrolled at St. Paul's School. He would have been encouraged there to translate back and forth from Latin poetry to English poetry, but even his early translations show remarkable creativity and intellectual force.

Milton may, like Alexander Pope, have lisped in numbers: any childish rhymes he may have remembered quickly evolved into original and mature poetry. He certainly translated and wrote original poetry from a very early age. Encouraged by tutors who were themselves grammarians, parsers of ancient Greek poetry, or poets, and encouraged by a father who was himself a not very good poet but a better composer (Campbell, "Shakespeare" 102), Milton seems fated to have written learned, musical poetry from his childhood on. Since John Milton Senior was an occasional poet, his son certainly associated voice or musical instrumentation and composing with verse. Composing music, singing, playing musical instruments, and writing poetry were fused in his imagination, in what he identified as "Sphear-born harmonious Sisters, Voice, and Vers" ("At a Solemn Musick" 2).

He could write poetry in Greek, Latin, Italian, and English, and he practiced writing in each of those four languages. The study of Greek was still exotic or esoteric in the early 1600s, since it was the language learned for study of the New Testament or for recently translated works by Plato or Euripides; but Latin was the universal language of the Renaissance, the language of schoolboy exercises and college disputations, the language of international religion and theological writing, and the language of diplomacy. Milton's Latin poetry was accomplished and sensitive, if not especially original, since his Latin vocabulary and idioms were restricted to those classical or "pure" Latin authors such as Ovid, Horace, or Vergil. Milton's first published volume of poetry, the 1645 *Poems*, was divided in half, with English and Italian poetry in one volume separated from the Latin poetry in another. The two volumes even had two independent title pages. There is evidence that Milton himself preferred to write poetry in his mother tongue. Like most of us, he seems to have been more comfortable writing in his native English than he was in writing in Latin, but the choice between writing in Latin or in English was open to him, and in many ways his Latin compositions were as valuable to him as his English poetry or correspondence, for his personal satisfaction, for his career, and for his reputation. His Latin poetry and prose served to establish him as an international player, as a poet or diplomatic agent or correspondent. When he participated in the meetings of Italian academies in Florence, for instance, Milton read poems he had written in Latin, not English. Milton composed some of his most revealing poetry, such as "*Epitaphium Damonis*" or "*Ad Patrem*," in Latin, and he wrote some of his most revealing letters in the ancient language. Modern readers who have no Latin lose quite a bit of Milton's poetry (and prose, for that matter).

Milton is remarkable for his friendships, a number of which with men and women, young and old, continued for many years. His mentor Thomas Young remained in correspondence with his pupil for many years, as did his St. Paul's schoolmaster, Alexander Gil. But Milton's most celebrated friendship was with his classmate from St. Paul's School, Charles Diodati. The two young men remained close even after Charles had gone up to Oxford and Milton had gone to Cambridge. Milton wrote to his friend in Latin and Diodati sometimes replied in Greek. He did write to Milton to "[l]ive, laugh, enjoy your youth and the present hour; and stop studying the zeals and licenses and recreations of the wise men of old, meanwhile wearying yourself" (French, *Life Records* 1.105). Milton may well have been the thoughtful one ("Il Penseroso") to his friend's happy-go-lucky one ("L'Allegro").

Charles Diodati was the son of a physician and the product of a distinguished Italian-English Protestant family with connections to the Protestant city of Geneva, Switzerland, where Charles's theologian uncle Jean (or Giovanni) Diodati lived, and with the family seat of Lucca, not far from Florence, in Italy. By all evidence, Charles was John Milton's soul-mate. To Diodati (the name means "gift of God") Milton wrote Latin elegies in the style of Ovid, in which he poured out his feelings about life, love, and death. After Milton received word of Diodati's premature death – while Milton was in Italy – the eventual poetic result was the moving elegy "*Epitaphium Damonis*," in which Diodati is given the mythical name of Damon, one of two young men classically famous for their friendship; Milton is his implied other half, Pythias. Milton's friendship with Diodati has been called "homoerotic" or unconsciously homosexual, but, since the two young men traded stories about heterosexual attraction, it is difficult to say with any certainty that Milton was even what is called today a repressed homosexual, especially since Charles Diodati was the only man with whom he had such a deep friendship.

Milton was also a notable friend to his own schoolmasters, such as Alexander Gil, to the bookseller George Thomason and his wife Catherine, and to a number of his pupils, such as his own nephews, Edward and John Phillips, sons of his sister Anne, both of whom wrote about and received the support of their uncle. Milton's friendships with the Italians he had come to know through the Diodati family – men such as Carlo Dati and Lucas Holste, Vatican Librarian – resulted in correspondence bordering the intimate. The diplomat Hermann Mylius, who knew Milton in the turbulent early 1650s, when Milton was in the process of going blind, seems to have grown more and more respectful of Milton's integrity, until they grew to be friends. Milton's friendly tutorial with the young Quaker Thomas Ellwood – the blind poet being read to and helping the younger man with his own studies – was remembered fondly in Ellwood's autobiography. And Milton's friendship with his co-worker and fellow poet Andrew Marvell resulted in Marvell's eloquent poetic defense of Milton and *Paradise Lost* published with the poem in 1674. Out of courageous loyalty to their friendship, Marvell pleaded for Milton's life and his pension in Parliament after the Restoration, when Milton was being publicly excoriated as a regicide. Marvell's loyalty was especially courageous because it put him, Marvell, under suspicion as well, and it was admitted to the parliamentary record when Marvell, as a Member of Parliament, defended his friend.

Milton abroad

When Milton left for his own grand tour of the continent, in May, 1638, he was planning to visit France (briefly), Italy, and Greece. The pattern of his travel seems to have been at least partly motivated by the need to search for the classical roots of Greek and Roman civilization and return to the countries of Cicero and Ovid, or Plato and Euripides. He did not make it to Greece, probably because he felt compelled to return to England, for political reasons, before his allotted travel time was up. But, from reading Milton's later prose and poetry, one gets the impression that he drank up and absorbed Italian culture, as if he lived life more intensely in that country, where he knew the language, the literature, the history, and perhaps even the art. Michelangelo had, for instance, been the only artist to create a synthesis of Christian history in one work of art – the ceiling of the Sistine Chapel – comparable to what Milton would attempt in *Paradise Lost*.

To get abroad, he made what was then a comparatively dangerous sea and land journey from London to Paris, where he met the famous legal historian and poet Hugo Grotius, whose printed works would take up about as much library shelf-space as the twentieth-century *Columbia Edition of the Works of John Milton*. From Paris he aimed toward Italy, through Nice to Genoa, Livorno, and then from Pisa to Florence, which was apparently the main target for his European stay. There in Florence, Milton tells us, he met the aged Galileo, under house arrest by the Inquisition. The meeting between the potentially great English poet and the greatest Italian astronomer has always been fascinating to contemplate. Milton went to meetings of one Florentine academy that were also attended by Vincenzo Galilei, one of the astronomer's illegitimate children (named after Galileo's father, the musical theorist Vincenzo). The youthful Galileo Galilei had been a novice at the Benedictine monastery of Vallombrosa, mentioned by Milton in *Paradise Lost*. Various Italian and Swiss members of Charles Diodati's family were associated with Galileo. Milton was to own a copy of Galileo's *Dialogo . . . sopra i due massimi sistemi del mondo, tolemaico e copernicano* ("Dialogue concerning the Two Chief World Systems – Ptolemaic and Copernican"), which had been banned in Italy since 1633, so he knew of Galileo's stature as something of a martyr to the intolerance of the Inquisition (Campbell, *Chronology* 61). Milton would later re-create the view through Galileo's telescope in *Paradise Lost*, describing

> the Moon, whose Orb
> Through Optic Glass the *Tuscan* Artist views
> At Ev'ning from the top of *Fesole*,
> Or in *Valdarno*, to descry new Lands,
> Rivers or Mountains in her spotty Globe.
> (1.287–91)

The Tuscan artist is Galileo, called an artist probably for his skill in designing optical instruments. Galileo is pictured in an observatory in Fiesole, an uphill suburb of Florence, or in Valdarno, the valley of the Arno river. What he sees and what Milton apparently saw through the telescope is what appears to be a new world on the moon, with newly-discovered mountains and craters that make it seem to be more like the earth and less of a perfectly circular heavenly body than was previously thought. Milton had a great deal to talk about with Galileo, who wrote about imagery in Italian chivalric epics as well as mathematical theory. Both men went blind in their senior years, and both men were certainly rebels, socially, scientifically, politically, and theologically.

The English poet and potential political activist Milton visited much of Italy, and there is evidence that he stirred up trouble – not just by visiting Galileo but by questioning tenets of the Roman Catholic religion, the religion of the state, on the Pope's home turf. Milton went to Rome in October of 1638. He was sufficiently well-known in scholarly circles to be welcomed at what is now known as the Vatican Library by the Pope's librarian, Lucas Holste, and he was invited to a spectacular performance of a comic opera sponsored by Cardinal Francesco Barberini, advisor to his uncle, Pope Urban VIII, and chief hospitality expert and collector of converts for the Roman church. The set designs for the musical production were by Gianlorenzo Bernini, perhaps the best-known sculptor and architect of his baroque age. Milton must have been reminded of the performance of his own masque (later known as *Comus*) in Ludlow.

Milton was also entertained in Rome by Jesuit priests (the Jesuits then and still have been traditionally the best-educated, most liberal, and most tolerant of priestly orders) who probably had as their goal to entice English Protestants to convert to Roman Catholicism. By his own account, Milton resisted so successfully that he was later warned that the Jesuits had plotted against him, perhaps to the point of arranging that he be killed should he return to Rome (he did, nevertheless).

Milton's Italian travels included a visit to Naples, a seat of ancient Roman culture ruled in the 1630s by the Spanish, where he met Giovanni Battista Manso, the Marquis of Villa, biographer of and friend to the poet Torquato Tasso, the author of the chief religious epic of his era, *Jerusalem Delivered*. Manso complimented Milton's bearing, his intellect, his grace, his charm, and his manners, while deploring his outspoken Protestantism (*Riverside* 175), and the older gentleman escorted Milton through Neapolitan ruins, perhaps showing him Mt. Vesuvius and the nearby Phlegrian Fields, sulphuric tar-pits supposed to resemble the landscape of Hell or the entrance to Hades supposed by ancient writers to be at Phlegethon (compare Vergil, *Aeneid* 6.551). Without his Protestantism, Manso wrote in a commendatory poem, Milton would have been an angel, rather than just an Anglo-Saxon.

Marriage and Divorce

Not long after Milton returned to England, he married. A good case might be made, using Milton as an example, that one should not marry a woman whose father owes you money. On June 11, 1627, when his son John was 18, John Milton Sr. had loaned Richard Powell the sum of £300, creating in the process a bond for £500, which, at 8 percent, provided a yearly interest income of £24, payable in two increments assigned to John Milton Jr. The father was setting his son up for a kind of premature inheritance or endowment, the equivalent of a trust fund, but the son had to collect the interest payments or rents. There may have been social problems as well. Richard Powell was a country squire who owned land not far from the ancestral Milton holdings in Oxfordshire, and there is evidence that perhaps Richard and surely his wife Anne looked down on the middle-aged man who was to become their future son-in-law; he might be, as Edward Phillips put it, "a blot in their Escutcheon" (*Riverside* 23).

In May of 1642, when Milton was an oldish bachelor of 33, hoping to collect his semi-annual payment of £12 at Forest Hill, Richard Powell's Oxfordshire manor, he was apparently smitten or resmitten with an attraction to Powell's eldest daughter, Mary, and according to Milton's nephew Edward Phillips's tongue-in-cheek account, "home he returns a Married-man, that went out a Batchelor" (*Riverside* 23). Mary had ten brothers and sisters, all of whom may have descended on Milton's house in Aldersgate Street house in London for the wedding festivities in July.

The Civil War was beginning. There must have been tensions

between Milton the Puritan sympathizer and his Royalist in-laws. By August, Mary's friends had petitioned her new husband to allow his wife to come back to Oxfordshire for the remainder of the summer. She then disappeared from his life for three years, during which time the Powell family and Milton's brother Christopher declared for the king's side. Milton was to write four tracts – *The Doctrine and Discipline of Divorce, Tetrachordon, The Judgement of Martin Bucer Concerning Divorce* (a translation of Bucer's Latin and commentary on it), and *Colasterion* – all advocating divorce on the grounds of what might today be called mutual incompatibility, or irreconcilable differences, or extreme neglect or cruelty. Milton also contended that the state, and not the church, should judge whether divorces should be granted. Politics inevitably intruded on marriage and family relations, and it wasn't until 1645, when Milton was actively studying polygamy and planning a potentially bigamous marriage to the daughter of a Dr. Davis, that Mary 's family engineered a reconciliation, with the wife "making Submission and begging Pardon on her Knees before him" for her husband to take her back (*Riverside* 24). Wife and husband were reconciled, even after her desertion, and the marriage produced several children. Begetting them would be an unthinkable psychological burden for the idealist Milton if he did not love his wife. Some bitterness over being deserted or betrayed seems to have remained with Milton for the rest of his life (it is perhaps reflected in the character Samson's anger at his wife Dalila's betrayal and desertion), and, despite the fact that most of the Powell clan (father and mother and at least five children) moved in to Milton's London house in the Barbican during the hotter phases of the Civil Wars, Milton seems not to have been reconciled to his sometimes deadbeat father-in-law (Richard Powell was often late on payments, and he defaulted on various loans) or his stereotypical shrewish mother-in-law. Mrs. Powell was probably the one who characterized him as "harsh" and "choleric" in a court deposition recorded in July of 1651, when she was wrangling for part of her by then dead husband's estate still controlled by Milton (Parker 398) – an unpleasant legal statement which was recorded at a time when Anne Powell's daughter, Mary Powell Milton, was pregnant with the last of their children, Deborah. As was sadly commonplace in the seventeenth century, Deborah's birth contributed to her mother Mary's death – at the age of 27 – three days after Deborah was born, on May 2, 1652. Family matters when his mother-in-law deposed against him in 1651 must have been oppressive for the blind Milton and his fatally pregnant wife.

It is hard to imagine now, but Milton was known for four things during his lifetime, none of which had anything to do with poetry:

- his opinions on divorce, which were notorious in a time of legally enforced monogamy for being egregiously wrong-headed;
- his attacks on the church hierarchy of prelates or Anglican bishops allied with the King;
- his defense of the legal execution of King Charles I, called "regicide" ("king-killing") by opponents of the practice;
- his position within the Interregnum parliamentary government of Oliver Cromwell, which was Secretary for Foreign Tongues (diplomatic interpreter and translator; interrogator of political prisoners; censor).

Most of the opponents who spoke out against Milton the divorcer had no idea that he was a poet or an elegant stylist in prose – at least not until he attacked them, mercilessly, in magnificent, colorful language, rich in imagery and crammed with allusion. In *Colasterion*, Milton ruthlessly attacked an anonymous hack who had written against one of the divorce tracts, calling him an ignorant "serving man." Those who attacked Milton's antiprelatical tracts, such as Bishop Joseph Hall, himself an excellent prose stylist, were also subjected to Milton's withering ridicule, debated in the best Cambridge oratorical style. God help any controversialist who picked a fight with Milton and did not know his Latin grammar inside and out.

When Milton's divorce tracts were subjected to prepublication censorship, Milton responded with *Areopagitica*, the most elegant legal statement in favor of unlicenced printing ever written. As fate ironically had it, Milton himself in later life would become a censor: he would be asked in 1649 by Parliament to examine the royalist newspaper *Mercurius Pragmaticus*, becoming a kind of official censor and spy-catcher for the Interregnum government (Campbell, *Chronology* 101).

Milton as divorcer is much closer to modern tastes than to those of the mid-seventeenth century, since what he argued for in his divorce tracts – divorce or dissolution on the grounds of mutual incompatibility – has become common law in most free nations.

When King Charles I took what Milton considered to be too much power unto himself, beginning in the late 1620s, enforcing his monarchal power through his control of the bishops of the Church of England, Milton opposed what he thought the illegal bond between church and state embodied in the autocratic, king-kissing, church rule of the Archbishop of Canterbury, William Laud. Milton attacked church governance, church ritual, even church robes or vestments, trying to break what he considered to be the false idols, or icons, he found in Laud's version of the English church. Laud, with the king behind him, enforced harsh policies with harsh penalties for disobeying them – mutilation and public whippings for those who dissented. During the decade of the 1630s, Milton became thoroughly radicalized, even though he had certainly been a monarchist church-supporter in his youth, celebrating bishops in Latin elegies and scorning the Gunpowder Plot in a series of Latin poems because it threatened to destroy the monarchy of James I. By 1638 and the publication of "Lycidas," he expressed bitter contempt for the corruption of the church and the academic system that prepared young men like himself to join become insincere and money-grubbing clergymen; by 1638 he had clearly joined the antiprelatical camp.

The political issues were divine-right kingship, the power of the people as expressed through parliaments, and the control of religious practices – what would later be labeled as "freedom of conscience" or "freedom to worship." As Thomas Corns has characterized it, "the authorial voice" in Milton's antiprelatical tracts "is violent, undeferential and implacable" (*Regaining* 128). Milton's violent, partial, opinionated voice was as it needed to be in such dangerous times. Milton was fortunate to escape being pilloried in stocks in public view, or whipped in the street, or having his ears cut off, as did William Prynne in 1634. Prynne's ears were cut again, even closer to the bone, for another offence against Archbishop Laud, in 1637. By 1642 Civil War had begun in England, and by January 30, 1649, the Parliamentary forces were to gain enough power to hold a public trial and then cut off the head of King Charles I of England, whom many people still considered to be a divinely anointed monarch. For a century that began with an entrenched theory of divine kingship, it was indeed a momentous thing for Parliament to meet and decide to cut off the head of a king.

But by 1649 Milton was defending the process of executing the

King. Milton pictured himself as an iconoclast, breaking the idol of kingship – what was called "the sacred portraiture of his majesty" – just as he had tried to break the idols of Laud's church. Though Milton entered the controversy as a private citizen, his talents as a propagandist were quickly recognized by the chief officers of the Parliament, and he was hired as a kind of public defender of the new Parliamentary government, a military oligarchy under the control of the Lord Protector, Oliver Cromwell.

Early Work

Milton was not a famous poet until the very end of his life, even though he made every effort to announce himself as at least a promising poet while he was reciting poetry in the Florentine academies in 1638, and in the presentation of his 1645 *Poems*. His first publisher, Humphrey Moseley, did recognize his talents and compared him favorably with Edmund Spenser, but for the most part the voice of the quiet little 1645 volume was drowned out by the political noise surrounding the beginning of the Civil Wars. The early Milton was a muted Milton. His masque, now popularly known as *Comus*, was anonymously published in 1637, and the elegy "Lycidas" was itself first buried in an unnoted memorial volume of Greek, Latin, and English poetry devoted to the memory of Edward King in 1638, *Justa Edovardo King, Naufrago* ("Poems to the Memory of Edward King, Ship-wrecked"). Not even "On Shakespeare," written in 1630 and first published in the 1632 Second Folio of Shakespeare's works, received much notice as signed "by JM." It is only by hindsight that we can establish a connection between the two greatest English poets of the seventeenth century. But, all the while that he was being ignored by most important people of his own generation, Milton was building his own monument, in a process that Richard Helgerson has cleverly labeled the creation of a "self-crowned laureate," which in Milton's case was "based exclusively on the functions of poet and prophet" (Helgerson 280). Recently, Joseph Wittreich and Martin Evans have investigated the extent to which the author has not only survived but has been reborn by self-construction.

Like many gentlemen, Milton was hesitant to announce his name on title pages. The first publication of his masque was anonymous, as were some of his prose pamphlets. He was not celebrated as a poet until well after *Paradise Lost* was published, and not lionized or worshiped as a great English poet until the first or second generation after his death, when *Paradise Lost* was published in a folio edition in 1688. By 1688 Milton might be pictured with a laurel wreath around his head, as the best poet of his nation, but he wasn't pictured that way when alive.

Milton and the Commonwealth

From about 1645, if not before, on until the end of his life, Milton was caught up not in poetry but in prose polemic – the public written defense of various political and theological and legal positions in which he fervently believed. Soon after 1645, his talents as a vociferous debater caught the eye of Parliamentary forces, and he was hired to provide high-quality propaganda for Cromwell's government. He was retained for his linguistic skills eventually, as much as for his debating skills. On his own, he had written four sometimes vitriolic, usually elegant and learned tracts defending the then almost unthinkable practice of divorcing oneself from one's spouse: there are many more citations of Milton in contemporary publications as "divorcer" than as a poet. One thing led to another. His divorce tracts met the enmity of the censor; censorship annoyed the author; and the author then wrote most eloquently against the practice of prepublication censorship, in *Areopagitica*. Milton's short prose tract is still studied by legal scholars as the definitive defense of free speech in print, or, in the US, the first amendment to the Constitution. In its own time, *Areopagitica* was too learned, and too elegantly and beautifully written, perhaps, to make much of an impression on the general public. It was also at least 100 years ahead of its time in its progressive thinking. Its language and ideas would inform the revolutionary colonists Benjamin Franklin and Thomas Jefferson, with their emphasis on the freedom of the press, in the 1770s, but Milton's version of the freedom of the press is much less liberal than that envisioned by Franklin and Jefferson.

Milton's ideal government system, which can be over-simply represented as rule by an educated elite rather than by an inherited monarchy, is more appealing to modern taste than the image of a king or queen with life and death power over a cringing public, but

Milton did not believe in universal franchise (he may or may not have believed that women should have legal rights or own property or vote – we don't know for sure). He believed that some people were too ignorant to be allowed to rule, and he may have believed that some nations were too backward to govern their own countries – the Irish, for instance, were "murderous," Irish rebels were "abhorrent," and the Irish could be summed up as "Barbarians" (of course, the fact that the Irish were predominantly Catholic colored Milton's bad opinion of them). When Milton pictures Samson bringing down the temple of the worshipers of Dagon and in doing so destroying a multitude of Philistines, the Hebrew forces represented by Samson feel no pity for the death of idol-worshipers or infidels. And, though Milton could take the part of oppressed Protestants in the Piedmont region of Italy as they were being slaughtered by Roman Catholic military forces in his "On the Late Massacher in Piemont" (1652), we don't know whose side he might have taken if Roman Catholics were at the mercy of Protestant forces. Milton certainly believed in righteous anger as a legitimate moral force: there were times when the enemies of God just had to be punished. Milton's Samson declares of his victory at Ramath-lechi, "A thousand foreskins fell" (144), showing no remorse for having killed and mutilated 1,000 of his enemies in battle.

Milton wrote strongly in defense of various kinds of liberty – domestic (family) liberty, liberty to worship according to one's conscience, and political liberty as expressed in what he called "liberty of speaking" (*Yale* 1.669) or "the honest liberty of free speech" (*Yale* 1.804). But he also believed that the opposite of liberty was license – uncontrolled, wild, chaotic behavior – and that license should not be mistaken for liberty. Milton's word "liberty" is culturally restricted, as various critics have pointed out: liberty of the press does not preclude censorship, say, of Roman Catholic "untruths" (Illo).

Milton the Egoist

Samuel Taylor Coleridge marveled at the egoism of Milton the poet and the man.

> In the Paradise Lost – indeed in every one of his poems – it is Milton himself whom you see; his Satan, his Adam, his Raphael, almost his

Eve – are all John Milton; and it is a sense of this intense egotism that gives me the greatest pleasure in reading Milton's works. The egotism of such a man is a revelation of spirit. (*Table Talk* II.240–1; quoted in Wittreich, *Romantics* 277)

In this age of the disappearing author, on the one hand, and the *auteur* bleeding all over the page on the other, Milton stands out as his own man in his works, the ever-intrusive author, the author at the center. When I first read Milton, I confess to having been annoyed with his intrusiveness and his pervasive presence in his own works. Milton at one time or another seems very close to being his own Lady (in *Comus*), or his God, Adam, Eve, Jesus, or Samson. In saying this, I don't mean to imply that Milton the author is blasphemous in playing God, but I do imply that he is present, pervasively, in all of his important "good" characters and in some of his bad ones. He certainly sees himself in the role of blind poet, isolated, besieged, vulnerable, but strong in his weakness, in *Paradise Lost,* and yet again in *Paradise Regain'd* and *Samson Agonistes.* Coleridge says Milton is "almost his Eve," but I would argue that Milton is certainly in his Eve, to the extent that some critics assume that Eve is a being so forceful that she has an existence independent of Milton!

We could play this critical game to a ridiculous point. Obviously, many of the romantic critics, believing with Blake that Milton was of the devil's party without his knowing it, took Satan to be the most powerful character in *Paradise Lost*, but when we study the character from the perspective of Milton's theology, or if we apply the character found in *Paradise Regain'd* to the much more forceful figure of Milton's earlier epic, we see that part of the force of Satan is in the details of Milton's presentation. When Satan seems to argue from *Areopagitica*, or when Satan stops lying for a second and begins using the truth, we get confused or seduced into following him temporarily.

I may be wrong, but I see Belial as a figure of great fear to Milton, because Belial is the spectre of the failed and ineffectual intellectual – the person who thinks too much and never gets anything done. Obviously, Milton fought all his life against becoming such a person, yet he was an intellectual, an orator, a smooth talker, a charmer, and a lover of beauty – all characteristics of Belial. Such an intellectual, if you put a drink in his hand and "set women in his eye," becomes an emblem of the most insidious kind of evil, the charming sleazy politician, hollow but convincing, a master of seeming accomplishment, the embodiment of sloth. Ever the hard worker and the accomplisher, Milton most feared the effete intellectual within himself.

The Milton myth

Though Milton gave as good as he got in the various pamphlet wars fought over divorce, prelacy, and regicide, the man himself was by all accounts charming, witty (if a bit sardonic), physically attractive, intellectually impressive, formidable in his passive power even after he became completely blind. His friendships were notably loyal, and strangers such as Herman Mylius, seeing the blind diplomatic secretary for the first time, were immediately impressed that they were in the presence of "a man of the highest esteem" or "the great Milton" (translated in Campbell, *Chronology* 123, 124).

Milton married three times, and, except for Mary's desertion (perhaps politically motivated, or instigated by her mother), we hear of no complaints from his wives. The one bit of incriminating evidence we hear of his character within his household is in the uncertain and perhaps unreliable testimony of a housemaid about events that occurred about 11 years before her deposition – that young Mary was supposed to have said that she would just as soon see her father dead as married to Elizabeth Minshull, Milton's third wife as of 24 February 1663. We don't know which daughter, if any, might have said such a thing, Deborah being only 10 in 1663, and we don't know who might be to blame when a stepmother enters a household with adolescent stepdaughters two wives removed from their birth mother. We have the testimony of the maidservant, Elizabeth Fisher, that "his said children had made away with some of his books and would have sold the rest of his books to the dunghill women" (Parker 586). Since Deborah was so young, it was probably Mary who "had conceived a violent dislike for her father" (Parker 586), an enmity that might cause her to try to cheat him and sell his most precious possessions, his books. Milton himself was supposed to have called his daughters "unkind" in the process of issuing his nuncupative (orally delivered) will to his lawyer brother Christopher: "The portion due me from Mr. Powell, my former wife's father, I leave to the unkind children I had by her, having received not part of it; but my meaning is, they shall have no other benefit of my estate than the said portion and what I have besides done for them, they having been very undutiful to me" (quoted in Parker 647). Though Milton's will sounds vindictive, and though it was contested by Mary and Anne (Anne was "lame and almost helpless" at the time [Parker 648]), he may have been assigning the responsibility of collecting the Powell dowry, £1,000 never paid, to the Powell grandchildren – for which there is a certain ironic justification. The £1,000, according to Christopher Milton, was in the hands of the two daughters' grandmother and uncle and therefore might have been available to the two girls through the Powell side of the family.

In testimony to Deborah's later and more healthy relationship with her father, we have the evidence that at some point after his death she asked for and received various personal relics from her father's estate, including a lock of his hair, and we have the witness of Jonathan Richardson (1734) that the then schoolmistress Deborah burst into tears spontaneously when she saw her father's portrait, saying "'tis My Father, 'tis my Dear Father" (Richardson in Darbishire 229). This same Deborah reported that her father was "Delightful Company, the Life of the Conversation, and That on Account of a Flow of Subject, and an Unaffected Chearfulness and Civility" (Darbishire 229). Such is not the testimony of an abused child.

We do have the infamous picture created by Edward Phillips, that Milton "Condemn'd [at least two of his daughters] to the performance of Reading, and exactly pronouncing of all the Languages of what ever Book he should at one time or another think fit to peruse" (*Riverside* 28). Phillips notes how vexing this might have been to the daughters, even in a time during which women were restrained by a patriarchal household hierarchy, and modern readers might become annoyed with the very image of the patriarchal Milton imposing cruel duties on young women; but faithful service to a blind father would have been considered a daughter's duty in the 1660s, and Deborah, at least, retained enough of her father's literacy and love for learning to be willing and able to teach children herself. Aubrey reports that Deborah read to her father in Latin, Italian, French, and Greek (he first wrote "Hebrew" as well but crossed it out), and Aubrey did not record any objection to that process. He reports matter-of-factly that Deborah was her father's amanuensis and that her father taught her "Latin, & to read Greeke" to him in his blindness (*Riverside* 2). Deborah, who became Deborah Clarke by marriage, also inherited her father's phenomenal memory, apparently, and she was able to recite long passages out of Homer and Vergil, many years after having memorized them. The image of the blind Milton dictating *Paradise Lost* to his daughters, whether or not any one of them was his amanuensis, has become a part of the mythology of the poet and is the subject of a painting by a Hungarian artist now hanging on a stairway in the New York Public Library. Whether the image is of patriarchal tyranny or familial cooperation is still hotly debated.

Milton had women friends throughout his career, some of whom, as with Lady Ranelagh, mother of one of his pupils, were quite well-read and even learned. It may have been that the Lady Frances Egerton, Countess of Bridgewater, who seems to have owned a copy of George Herbert's *The Temple* and Ben Jonson's *The New Inn* (Brown 33), persuaded her husband John Egerton, Earl of Bridgewater, to commission a masque from the young Cambridge poet John Milton. Milton celebrated his friendship with Catherine Thomason, wife of George Thomason, bookseller and collector, in a memorial sonnet, Sonnet 14, "When Faith and Love" (*Riverside* 253–4). Though none of his wives was notably well-educated, Mary, at least, was literate and wrote in her own family Bible (Campbell, *Chronology* 88), and his last wife, Elizabeth Minshull Milton, was certainly articulate and voluble with anyone who talked with her about her husband after his death: she was sensitive enough to remember that her husband did not like the work of the philosopher Thomas Hobbes. Modern psychological critics have assigned a very noticeable feminine (if not "homoerotic" as according to John Shawcross [chapter 3]) side to Milton's personality, and, on balance, Milton's reputation has held up well under the pressure of early feminist criticism, to the point where Joseph Wittreich could title a book about the subject *Feminist Milton* with impunity. Most modern Milton critics would agree that their man was in touch with his feminine side, and no biographer has accused Milton of being a misogynist.

Though Milton the man had a sardonic and sarcastic wit, Aubrey describes him as "Of a very cheerfull humour" (*Riverside* 3) and "Extreme[ly] pleasant in his conversation, & at dinner, supper &c: but Satyricall" (*Riverside* 3). Even Anthony à Wood, an early biographer politically inimical to Milton, wrote that "His deportment was affable, and his gate [gait] erect and manly, bespeaking courage and undauntedness" (*Riverside* 17). Samuel Hartlib, without an ax to grind in defending or satirizing Milton, described him as "a personable man and versed in all learning especially Civil Law and Histories" and as someone who was "a universal philologus, historian, civilian [student of civil law]" (Campbell, *Chronology* 147). The testimonies to Milton's good humor, affability, and companionability are so common that it is hard to see him as a dark-humored or moody and unpleasant person – even though he was a terror to his political opponents.

By the time Milton was in college, he seems to have been of a very light complexion (too little sun, while reading books?), to the point where he was nicknamed "the Lady of Christ's." Samuel Johnson, the great literary critic, an early and politically biased biographer of Milton, put it this way:

> Milton has the reputation of having been in his youth eminently beautiful, so as to have been called the Lady of his college. His hair, which was of a light brown, parted at the foretop, and hung down upon his shoulders, according to the picture which he has given of Adam. He was, however, not of the heroic stature, but rather below the middle size, according to Mr. Richardson, who mentions him as having narrowly escaped from being 'short and thick.' He was vigorous and active, and delighted in the exercise of his sword, in which he is related to have been eminently skillful. His weapon was, I believe, not the rapier but the backsword [a sword with only one cutting edge], of which he recommends the use in his book on education.
>
> His eyes are said never to have been bright; but, if he was a dexterous fencer, they must have been once quick.
>
> His domestic habits, so far as they are known, were those of a severe student. He drank little strong drink of any kind, and fed without excess in quantity, and in his earlier years without delicacy of choice. In his youth he studied late at night; but afterwards changed his hours, and rested in bed from nine to four in the summer, and five in the winter. The course of his day was best known after he was blind. When he first rose he heard a chapter in the Hebrew Bible, and then studied till twelve; then took some exercise for an hour; then dined; then played on the organ, and sung, or heard another sing; then studied to six; then entertained his visitors till eight; then supped, and after a pipe of tobacco and a glass of water, went to bed. (Johnson 421)

Although Johnson abhorred Milton's politics, his account of Milton's appearance and habits may be better informed by eyewitness and hearsay testimony than a modern biographer's re-creation. One can see in Johnson's picture of the organization of Milton's waking time that he wasted no time, and that he was devoted to reading and studying, especially study of biblical texts. Music is there, singing and organ-playing and listening to performers, as is sociability. Mind-bending strong drink such as distilled liquor is not, but wine or beer might have been permitted, since we know that Milton had convivial glasses of wine with students. Exercise remained a part of Milton's life even after he went blind, and Johnson's estimate of an hour a day, for walking or some other form of strenuous aerobic activity, seems accurate for such a well-organized man as Milton.

Milton depended on others to take dictation, especially after his blindness caused him not to be able to write his own name accurately on a page. He liked reading and being read to, and he liked learning and teaching through recitation, memorization, and reading aloud. After his blindness, he seems to have depended on what must have seemed at times to have been a home factory of scribes and amanuenses, people taking dictation and sometimes being taught in return for the various services. The handwriting of a number of different scribes, many of them all but anonymous, occurs in the disputed manuscript of the theological treatise attributed to Milton, *De Doctrina Christiana*, "On Christian Doctrine." If as many as 15 different handwriting types occur there, the home factory of scribes must have included most people who came through the Milton's front door, plus his students, his daughters, and anyone who could write.

Class-consciousness

The social class of the Miltons, father and son, is hard to define, because they were prosperous tradesmen and real-estate dealers, but at the same time well-educated gentlemen. John Milton remained frugal enough so that he could support himself throughout his life from the investment income that his father's business dealings provided for him. Like a landed aristocrat, he did not *have* to work for a living. Milton was by all accounts careful of his money, if not somewhat miserly except for book purchases, and he managed to live on whatever his interest earnings, his school-teaching, or his public service provided. From an early age, he had the luxury to aspire to be that most useless and impractical thing, a poet, though he had at all times to keep an eye on his investments, to make sure rents were paid and interest payments were made to him on time. There is evidence that he paid for the tutoring of his daughters in languages as well as for their vocational training as seamstresses. The legal records of Milton's father and Milton himself are full of chancery court wrangling for money – suits and countersuits over percentages of property earnings. The legal records indicate that the Milton men, the father and both sons, were well-trained in keeping hold of their rental properties and their invested funds: John Sr., the poet's brother Christopher, and John Jr. were all well-off landholders when they died, despite the various misfortunes of the Civil Wars.

If Milton felt socially insecure at St. Paul's School or Christ's College, Cambridge, because he was surrounded in those privileged schools by students most of whom would have been of noble and wealthy families, neither his school exercises, his correspondence, nor his poetry show it. Instead they project self-confidence bordering on arrogance, as if Milton had already graduated from Cambridge and was therefore entitled to sign his name with "Gent." after it.

In 1647, however, Milton was satirized for writing on divorce in a broadside snottily titled *These Tradesmen are Preachers* (Campbell, *Chronology* 92), and he was described by a foreign diplomat as "not a nobleman but at least a gentleman" (Campbell, *Chronology* 118). As I have said, the country squire Royalist family of the Powells probably looked down on their tradesman son-in-law, despite his intellectual brilliance. And Milton himself looked down on serving-men, undignified college students, and, less frequently, on what Shakespeare called "unlettered hinds" or "rude mechanicals."

When Milton heaped scorn on his political opponents, he was not above using social slurs mixed in with other vitriolic labels, as when he called the anonymous author of the pamphlet that produced his own pro-divorce pamphlet *Colasterion* a "serving-man," labeling him according to his lack of education and his social position. Milton certainly considered himself a member of the intellectual elite, by virtue of his education, and his Cambridge degree did entitle him to call himself "John Milton, Gentleman." When he was outside England, however, he would sign himself "John Milton, Englishman."

Nationality was more important to him than was social rank.

Milton was always a master of irony, expressed in clever reversals in plot or in word-play. In about 1653, after he had gone blind and when he was in the process of writing the *Defensio Secunda*, his second defense of himself and his public conduct, Milton included a wonderfully mischievous and funny poem among his Latin prose, "Gaudete scombri," which can be translated as "Mackerels, rejoice!" The mackerels in question are the fish whose corpses – as freshly caught fish – would be wrapped in the pages of the books of Milton's rival's most recently published work, because the pages are so worthless. Here is my loose translation of Milton's rarely examined Latin poem:

> Rejoice mackerels, and other fish
> Who live in freezing inlets in the winter;
> Because that good old knight, Salmasius,
> Free with paper, becomes sad about your fate;
> To clothe your nakedness, he will make dresses
> Bearing the coats of arms, name, and achievements
> Of Claude Saumaize; so that in the fish stalls,
> You all may wear his paper livery
> As minions of his knightliness – a prize to those
> Who fill boxes and wipe their noses on their sleeves.

Milton is making fun of a pretentious opponent, the great scholar Claude Saumaise, known by his Latin name Salmasius, by characterizing his books as just so much wrapping for dead fish. The joke is worked out perfectly: The phrase "Gaudate scombri" sounds funny to begin with, in Latin, perhaps a parody of the famous college drinking song, "Gaudeamus igitur"; the mackerels are from the cold waters where they would actually be fished for; Salmasius becomes a ridiculous Don Quixote showing off meaningless diplomas and coats of arms; and the fishmongers are so preoccupied (and uncouth) that they wipe their noses on their sleeves. The poem is genuinely funny, but here it is incongruously placed in the middle of a serious attack on the monarchist Salmasius. Milton the poet with a very keen sense of humor emerges in the midst of political controversy. The poem is characteristic of the surprising Milton: in the midst of one mode, polemic prose debate, he shifts into another mode, that of satiric poetry (in learned Latin).

The Nativity Ode

At the age of 21, Milton composed a series of brilliantly organized, perfectly rhymed stanzas as a kind of birthday present for the infant Jesus. Composition was apparently very rapid. In a Latin verse letter written to Charles Diodati, Milton describes the process of quickly composing the poem, before daylight on Christmas Day, in a burst of poetic inspiration at a numinous time of year – a time of great spiritual energy. Milton as poet conceives of himself as beside himself, as if he were transported in time to Bethlehem and as if he were delivering his poem as a present to the Christ child, in person and to the manger, as if he were one of the three Magi or the three kings who followed the star to Bethlehem.

The ode on the nativity of Jesus is Milton's first obviously great poem, not like countless other Christmas-card poems of celebration, whether ode or hymn It summarizes a poetic tradition, but it also says new things in new ways, and it is poetically exciting, presenting a new and unique voice in English poetry – more like Spenser than Donne, to be sure, but not at all an imitation of Spenser, or of Marlowe or Shakespeare either, though Milton had probably read Chaucer, Spenser, Marlowe, Sidney, Joshua Sylvester, the Fletcher brothers, and Shakespeare by the time he was 21.

Like most of Milton's poetry, the Nativity Ode (it is identified by Milton as a hymn as well as an ode, and it has a proem or poetic prologue and then tells the story of the Nativity) is intensely personal as well as an anonymous and genuinely "humble" offering at the birth of Christ. Milton felt obliged to write to Diodati confessionally, to tell his friend about how the English poem was conceived and written, and then to publish the poetic letter to his friend in the same volume of poems that contained the Nativity Ode, as if to create and then solve a puzzle of interpretation for the sensitive reader of the ode. Milton writes his own notes to his own poem, to advise future editors on how to interpret his early work, or to control the response of future readers. This kind of authorial interference will become a hallmark or signature of the poet.

The poem itself is in the festive mood of Christmas. It is exuberant and joyful, fast-paced, playful; it celebrates creativity. It presents a parade of vivid images in beautiful language rigidly ordered by the stanza pattern. Milton has already mastered the art of writing in stanzas as intricate as those in which Spenser wrote *The Faerie Queene*. In homage to Spenser, Milton even includes an Alexandrine line (six stressed syllables in iambic rhythm) at the ends of stanzas. As in Spenser, the rhyme never seems forced, the language is rich in imagery appealing to most of the senses, and the verbal harmonies or combined word sounds are rich, varied, and sensuous.

The Nativity Ode is not a picture-postcard nativity scene or crêche with the usual *santons* or holy figures – the family of Jesus, the Wise Men, or the shepherds – in attendance (where is Joseph, for instance?). As a Protestant poet intensely aware of the religious power of imagery, Milton avoids common or sentimental pictures of the manger. The Virgin Mary is there, abstractly, as the "wedded Maid, and Virgin Mother," but her image is not emphasized; and the infant Jesus is compared with the infant Hercules, strong enough in his cradle to strangle serpents (or Satan in the Serpent). The fierceness of the infant is what is emphasized, not the tenderness of the babe or manger scene. And for Milton the Nativity is not just the time of birth: it is the time when evil spirits and false gods are cast out, during the "cessation of the oracles" that the earliest Church Fathers had identified, in rewriting pagan history.

When the infant Christ is not himself, in Milton's imagery he is the god Pan, by the etymology of his name the god of everything, or of all nature. Milton appropriates the pagan nature spirit Pan in the name of Christianity. Though such an appropriation of pre-Christian images was not unusual among Renaissance Protestant poets, identifying Christ as "the mighty *Pan*" who has come to speak with "Shepherds on the Lawn" (they appear to be English) seems outrageous, or at least provocative, even for 1629.

The *santons* of the usual manger scene are replaced with the energized figures of Christ as strong Hercules and Christ as the ever-present force of nature Pan. The poet, in another burst of energy, seems to picture himself or at least his heavenly muse outrunning the three Magi to present the ode as a birthday present to the Christ child. If the reader prefers to see Milton's Puritanism in his early poem, there is evidence of iconoclasm, of the poet's "inner light," and of the English author's need to express himself in English, not the Latin of Roman Catholic ceremony.

"L'Allegro" and "Il Penseroso"

Twin poems or echo poems, "L'Allegro" and "Il Penseroso" also present two sides of the question of personality, the schizophrenic splitting of one personality into two types of character. Which type of person will I be, they ask, thoughtful and melancholy, or happy and carefree? It may be too simple to speculate that the thoughtful personality is closer to the introspective and more solitary Milton, and that the carefree and spontaneous, crowd-loving personality may be closer to that of Milton's friend Charles Diodati, but that speculation at least provides a modern reader with the equipment to interpret the balancing act between the two poems. The poems are a kind of see-saw: when one type of personality is up, the other is down, yet the types balance one another, and they may both be incorporated into one balanced individual. Milton in person could be gregarious, fun-loving, sociable; yet the writing of poetry inclined one toward being solitary, moody, introspective, thoughtful, serious, and deep. The difference in personality remotely resembles the difference between Romeo and Mercutio.

The theory of humors might help a little here. The mercurial should be avoided. Melancholia should be balanced against sanguine, or phlegmatic behavior – black bile against blood or phlegm – in order for a personality to be temperate, balanced, with the humors in equilibrium within the body and the mind. Milton balances the masculine and feminine in the imagery, from the prophetic poet and scholar to the pensive nun, in gender as in personality type.

The poems are also balanced carefully, if not precisely, with one another: they do not stand alone. Each begins with the rejection of the way of life described in the other. Like Milton's standardized prolusions, college exercises disputing either side of an arguable position, the twin poems do not reach a resolution. In the end, day cannot be better than night; melancholy is as necessary to the well-rounded individual as is sanguine or phlegmatic behavior.

The twin poems are given Italian, musical names, but not for the sake of affectation. Milton does not seem to be impressing the reader with how many languages he knows. Instead, the Italian *allegro*, still used today in musical notation, is a richer, more evocative word than is the English "happy." And *penseroso* or *pensieroso* includes more than the English "pensive one." Thoughtful, melancholy, meditative, moody, and philosophical traits are all included in the term.

The twin poems, in another metrical experiment like the use of stanzas in the Nativity Ode, seem to be written in perfect-rhyme couplets for a reason. Milton is experimenting with another common verse form, one used by Christopher Marlowe in "Hero and Leander," pentameter couplets. His subject matter is not erotic, though. It is pastoral, evocative, pictorial, and musical all at the same time. Milton's poems seem to pick up the lyricism of the young Shakespeare at his very best in rhyme, as in the couplets Oberon or Titania use in describing fairyland or fairy events in *A Midsummer Night's Dream*. The descriptions of English rural or village life in "L'Allegro" and "Il Penseroso" are some of the most remarkable and precise in the English language, which is one reason why Handel set both poems to music in an oratorio devoted to bridging the gaps between Milton's words and pure musical sounds. Where Milton evokes the sounds of English church bells pealing, "When the merry Bells ring round," Handel re-creates them in a series of soprano arpeggios: the sound (believe me) is pure delight (try the 1992 Erato recording DDD 45377, with John Eliot Gardiner conducting).

The two poems mirror one another; as musical units, they echo one another; they represent two sides to one personality (or two complementary personality types); and they balance one another psychologically, in the sense that embracing both ways of life will make an individual well-rounded, temperate, or mentally healthy. Instead of resorting to academic stuffiness and repeating formulas used by Greek or Roman pastoral poets, they emulate the kinds of pastoral poetry written by English poets with a rural background and real knowledge of English shepherds, hedgers, milkmaids, or plowmen. Milton knows that English hedges are often clumps of hawthorn; he has heard the sound of the curfew call or "Belmans drousie charm" ("Il Penseroso" 83); and like a good budding scientist, he observes that the bee carries something that looks, at least, like a honey sac on its legs, while flying from flower to flower, humming its busy (beesy) hum. Milton's observation of the natural world is not sentimental, not condescending, not patronizing. The bee may be a wonderful insect, its honey a product valuable for the English economy; the plowman's work is dignified and necessary; and hawthorn makes an excellent hedge. Nut-brown ale, incidentally, still exists.

Like most of Milton's poetry and prose, the twin poems are auto-biographical without being obvious about it. The pensive man, for instance, reads Plato, studies classical tragedy, picks up the story of Canace from Chaucer, and thinks about the poet Orpheus as a role model. A modern biographer can prove that Milton did all of those things, even though, in the theoretical sense, Milton as author may be very difficult to define, and critics and biographers have argued for years whether or not his poetry is egocentric, on the one hand, or nearly anonymous on the other. The personality and firsthand observations of the poet are certainly present in the twin poems.

"Lycidas"

The great pastoral elegy focuses on personal and collective grief – that of Milton and his Cambridge classmates who grieved with him in poetry – over the death of one promising young man, Edward King, a classmate of Milton at Christ's College, Cambridge, who drowned under very unlucky circumstances during what should have been a routine crossing from Wales to Ireland. As someone who would take risks with his own travel, Milton anticipates his own danger in crossing water, and, like Shakespeare, he depicts the horrors of drowning and the wonders of the effects of drowning in sea changes accurately. Edward King's body is gracefully dismembered, if that is possible to conceive, by the waves.

Milton's poem is not unique, it is part of a collection of poems in English, Latin, and Greek published by King's friends at Cambridge. In an age which often celebrated the death of a Christian as an entrance to Heaven, memorial collections were not at all unusual, and Milton himself had celebrated famous bishops and members of his own family who had died in infancy in Latin memorial verse. The fact that King had died in a shipwreck struck his imagination, as did the fact that King's ship went down quickly and without any discernible cause. Edward King apparently lived as he died. A pious young theology student, he was supposed to have gone down with the sinking ship while praying on the deck, when the ship was within sight and presumably swimming distance of land.

Milton concentrates on King as a fellow student for the ministry, someone who emulated Christ as Good Shepherd, a pastoral figure.

King was also a fledgling poet, like Milton himself. Without embarrassment, Milton combined conventional devices of the Greek and Roman pastoral poem with Christian imagery. A pagan shepherd easily becomes a pastor, a minister, or a priest, taking pastoral responsibility for Christian souls with the love and the care that a good shepherd would show for his flock. The good shepherd also keeps the sheep from danger by penning them up at night, thereby protecting them against marauding wolves.

The shepherds of Greek pastoral poetry would also be singers, composers, artists who, divinely inspired, wrote hymns to the glory of God. As poet, then, Milton could picture himself both as an "uncouth swain" or neophyte writer and as a kind of Orpheus (plate 3). Since Orpheus, like Edward King, was torn apart (the one by crazed nymphs and the other by the sea), Milton as poet could display his own fear of death and its breaking apart of the body, and his sorrow for the loss of an artist (though Milton would not have used that word in the modern sense), both at the same time. It is difficult, as many critics have pointed out, to tell whether Milton is mourning for the death of his friend or for his own imagined death. In either case, the death of a young and promising poet is a sad event, worth celebrating in poetry.

Milton's poem is notable by contrast to the generally lame and conventional college verse of his Cambridge contemporaries also published in the *Justa Edovardo King* volume. Here are the opening couplets of one of two of John Cleveland's affectedly metaphysical poems:

> *I Like not tears in tune; nor will I prise*
> *His artificiall grief, that scannes his eyes:*
> *Mine weep down pious beads: but why should I*
> *Confine them to the Muses Rosarie?*
> *I am no Poet here; my penne's the spout*
> *Where the rain-water of my eyes run out*
> *In pitie of that name, whose fate we see*
> *Thus copi'd out in griefs Hydrographie.*
>
> (*Justa* 9)

The sarcastic modern reader might agree with Cleveland's "*I am no Poet here*" and laugh at the tears that become "*pious beads*" or the pen that ridiculously spouts the rainwater of Cleveland's tears. But

Plate 3   Bernardo Buontalenti, costume design for the poet Arion as Orpheus in the Medici wedding masque of 1589. Biblioteca Nazionale di Fisenze/ SCALA.

Cleveland and a number of the Christ's College poets published in *Justa Edovardo King* went on to publish independently as adults, and at least one of them, Joseph Beaumont, went on to write a now-forgotten epic poem, *Psyche*. Milton was certainly not the only fledgling poet at Cambridge. His elegy to King, however, was the most startlingly original poem in the collection, and it was probably given the last place in the volume in order to honor it as the final word on the death of King.

"Lycidas," when it was published under Milton's name in his 1645 *Poems*, became by hindsight a political statement about religious abuse, because it speaks out courageously and passionately, certainly representing courage in dissent in 1637, about the corruption then present in the Church of England as Milton perceived it. Milton's perception was that the young men who graduated from Cambridge and went into the ministry, actually a majority of the graduates, were quickly and easily corrupted into a life of collecting a salary (a "living" or a "benefice") in one place while living in another. Many clerics were, in effect, absentee landlords of the church, collecting money for duties not performed, and leaving parishes to the care of incompetent and often illiterate functionaries. The power of the bishops combined with corruption in granting benefices to favored younger sons of the aristocracy had created a negligent and unlearned church, from Milton's budding Puritan perspective, a church in which the "blind mouths" of corrupt priests were well-nourished but where the "hungry sheep," the parishioners, were not fed, spiritually and even intellectually speaking. Milton's political and theological anger at the English church as it existed in 1637 is shown by his interpretive headnote to "Lycidas" as it appeared in the 1645 *Poems*: "the Author . . . by occasion foretels the ruine of our corrupted Clergy then in their height." It was comparatively safe to make such an inflammatory statement in 1645; it had not been in 1637. Archbishop William Laud was executed in January of 1645: the "ruine" of the "corrupted Clergy" was embodied in the death of Laud.

Like any great poem, though, "Lycidas" has more than one level of significance. The death of a promising young person always causes reverberations of sorrow in the poet and the audience of a well-written elegy. A reader can interpret Milton's elegy on the level of the poet's response, "there but by the grace of God go I," and feel sorry for the death of the promising Edward King because such an unpredictable death can happen to any aspiring artist. The reader might also understand the poem through its pervasive allusion to the pastoral tradition, which works for the lawns of Cambridge grazed by sheep or for the nurturing of young minds by Cambridge tutors like the anonymous "old *Damætas*" of line 36. Milton adds another layer of semi-mythical English history, with the druids inhabiting islands near where King drowned. The appearance of druids on an English island Mona calls to mind the real but mystical Stonehenge or Tintagel or Glastonbury – English places with mysterious, ancient, religious, magical power. Modern students who have played Dungeons and Dragons, have seen the movies *Merlin* or *Monty Python and the Holy Grail*, or even those who have played elaborate fantasy computer games such as *Zelda*, can understand what Milton is doing in providing his poem with druids and mystical islands.

Controlling the entire poem is the Greek myth of Orpheus, like Edward King a poet torn apart because of a cruel trick of fate. Milton would prefer that English poets like Edward King and John Milton be identified with the mythological Orpheus, able to make boulders weep with the power of his song, words and music. But Orpheus was torn apart by a mob, "the rout that made the hideous roar," and Lycidas, Edward King, was dismembered by the merciless ocean.

Elegies in Latin and English

As the content of the book of commemorative poems celebrating the life and death of Edward King proves, it was possible for college-trained poets in the first half of the seventeenth century to write elegies or memorial poems in Greek, Latin, or English. Milton attempted to write a short memorial poem in English on the death of Christ, "The Passion," but he did not finish it, and in 1645 he declared the subject "to bc above the yeers he had, when he wrote it, and nothing satisfi'd with what was begun, left it [the poem] unfinisht." Scholars and critics have concluded that the subject of the Crucifixion was uncongenial to Milton, and perhaps it did not appeal to him simply because the image of Christ on the cross had become a commonplace icon for western European Roman Catholic artists. As a rule, Milton avoided images of the Madonna (as compared with the Protestant Mary, whom he will picture as more of a concerned mother than a saint, in *Paradise Regain'd*) or the crucified Christ in his poetry.

He certainly did not avoid dealing directly with the difficult subject of death. His funereal poetry in Latin and English memorialized

- an infant child in his own family, his sister's child;
- a marchioness;
- two Church of England bishops;
- a beadle (a Cambridge minor official); and
- a Cambridge vice-chancellor.

Despite his later writings against the institution of church rule by king-appointed bishops, Milton was respectful, at the age of 17, of the Bishop of Winchester, and he could write poems to the memory of the Bishops of Winchester and of Ely in good conscience. Milton could honor the memory of the famous sermonizer Lancelot Andrews, Bishop of Winchester, though he would later repudiate the practices of Andrews and other Anglican bishops.

Milton also joined in a post-mortem joke against a blue-collar worker associated with Cambridge University. The Cambridge University carrier (carter or teamster), Thomas Hobson, was celebrated after death by Milton and other Cambridge students in a series of humorous or satirical poems full of images of horses governed by "Hobson's choice" ("you can have any horse you want, just so long as it is the one nearest the stable door"). Milton enjoyed the subject so much that he wrote two or three (the authorship of the third is disputed) poems on the death of Hobson, each one full of outrageous puns about wagons, carriers, horses, gaits, and muddy passages.

"Here lieth one who did most truly prove, / That he could never die when he could move," wrote Milton in the second Hobson poem, giving us a picture of Hobson, who died at the age of 81, as a perpetual-motion machine while he was alive, too cantankerous to die while he could still get around. Milton exercised a function of his wit and cleverness in the Hobson poems that he thought beneath the level of decorum, most of the time, in epic poetry. He probably included Hobson among his published poems to show his future readers that he could indeed have a sense of humor, but without descending into obscenity.

Milton's Hobson poems are snobbish in that they look down on or laugh at menial labor from the perspective of a college student, but they do make us remember and see with fresh eyes a colorful scoundrel, a Falstaffian rogue who made a living outwitting or skinning or cheating bright undergraduates – a most unusual subject for the poetry of young university wits accustomed to writing elegies for bishops or college officials. Serious elegies were saved for the deaths of church dignitaries or prominent university officials; lighter memorial poems were written about men further down on the social scale. As with most of Milton's excursions into sub-genres of poetry, the Hobson poems are the best of their type, and they contain a Shakespearean eye for observing ordinary people, the kinds of people that Shakespeare called "nurse," or "drawer," or "clown." Hobson was a sophisticated clown.

Milton was keenly aware of when he was writing in the pastoral mode, when his poetry was elegiac in the sense of being funereal (as compared with writing in elegiac couplets, which is what Ovid did throughout his elegies celebrating love), and when he was writing on a lower level of understanding – a jokey, condescending level of understanding, as with the Hobson poems. His own strong sense of decorum would not allow him to mix the indecent with the decent, or violate the aura of seriousness, say, that protected the reputation of a dead bishop. When Milton himself labels his own nativity poem as both an ode and a hymn, he knows precisely what he is doing with both labels. As an ode, the Nativity Ode is descended from the odes of the Greek Pindar, celebrating the heroic man in noble verse designed for reciting at a public event, and from the more intimate odes of the Latin Horace, quietly celebrating decency and goodwill in ordinary human beings. Milton's audience would also be familiar with Christian hymns as sung in English churches, and the classical genre of hymns, as practiced by the Greek Callimachus, reverent paeans or hymns of praise celebrating Greek gods such as Dionysus or Ceres. Though Milton would not himself dare to write a psalm directly imitative of King David's, psalms being hymns in praise of the deity, he did during the course of his life translate a total of 17 of the biblical Psalms attributed to David; and hymns and psalms were intimately related in the minds of the English faithful. Since the word "ode" is derived from a Greek verb meaning "to sing," the relationships between odes and psalms, and between hymns and odes, and between the written and the sung, are obvious, especially to the synthesizing mind of a Christian humanist. And as the son of a composer and a musician and singer himself, Milton could think of himself as an inspired poet who could sing his own work and emulate the psalmist David. The roles of poet, singer, prophet, and civic leader were fused in what the character of a man should be. David was also the true version of what the pagan Orpheus or Arion should have been, the poet in touch with inspired truth.

Sonnets

Though Milton never wrote a sonnet cycle and though he never wrote a series of sonnets devoted to the real or imagined love of one woman (as did Petrarch or Philip Sidney), he did use the sonnet genre, in Italian and in English, to express sudden but deep emotional reactions – to death, to acts of atrocity, to friends and friendship, to eminent men and women he held in respect. He wrote occasional sonnets, sonnets celebrating a specific event; he wrote memorial sonnets; and (in Italian only) he wrote sonnets celebrating the beauty or the art of a woman. He even wrote one sonnet, that beginning "Captain or Colonel," designed to be tacked to his door in London to keep him from being attacked by soldiers passing by – because he was a poet!

Sonnets surrounded Milton's literary and intellectual life. His poetic idols – Dante, Petrarch, Sidney, Spenser, and Shakespeare – had all written sonnets. His predecessor as Latin Secretary for the Parliamentary government, George Weckerlin (1584–1653), was famous in his own country, Germany, for his sonnets. In histories of lyric poetry or encyclopedias of poetry and poetics, Milton is noted for having reintroduced the Italian sonnet rhyme scheme, *abba abba cde cde*, to English, but that rhyme scheme might just follow naturally from Milton's having written Petrarchan sonnets in Italian, though Milton always ends his sonnets written in Italian with an Anglicized couplet. He constantly experimented with 14-line iambic poems in Italian and in English by varying the rhyme scheme. He added a tail to one of his sonnets, "On the New Forcers of Conscience Under the Long Parliament," making it a caudal or caudate sonnet. He also practiced poetry in the longer, looser Italian form of the *canzone*, a

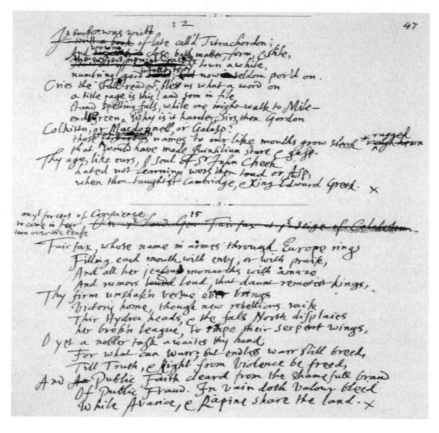

Plate 4 Two of Milton's sonnets in his handwriting, from the Trinity Manuscript. From S. L. Sotheby, *Ramblings in the Elucidation of the Autograph of Milton* (London: Thomas Richards, 1861). © British Library, London.

more elaborate lyric or emotional song sometimes built on sonnet structure. Some critics have called "Lycidas" a *canzone* – an extended lyric built on a looser metrical scheme than that of a canto or sonnet. Milton wrote an Italian *canzone* as well, dedicated to what seems to be an imaginary woman: he knew the form and was capable of using it in Italian and English. Milton used the *canzone* to approach something like free verse: in structure, at least, "Lycidas" is not unlike T. S. Eliot's "The Love Song of J. Alfred Prufrock."

Milton played with the sonnet form itself within its 14-line restriction. One of his Italian sonnets uses all A rhymes in its octave and all B rhymes in its sestet. In the 1645 *Poems*, Milton further confuses the interpreter of his sonnets by beginning a numbered sequence of Italian sonnets with an English sonnet, "To the Nightingale." Sonnets, he seems to be saying, should have no national and no linguistic boundaries.

Sonnets Milton wrote after he had become a public servant are often occasional poems with a wide scope of interest represented in the various occasions they celebrate. They can be laudatory (one praises General Thomas Fairfax; while another praises Milton's musical collaborator, the musician Henry Lawes; and still another Lady Margaret Ley, the daughter of a former Lord Chief Justice). They may represent a loving memorial (Sonnet 19, "Methought I saw my late espoused saint," to his dead wife who appears to him in a dream). They may be self-reflective (on his blindness or on time as the thief of his youth, or on his value to the country even in time of war). They may be collegial and modeled on the gracious Horatian ode (the sonnets he wrote to several of the young men whom he tutored). There are at least vestiges of sonnets within *Paradise Lost*. Some of Milton's sonnets are public utterances – verging on propaganda or journalism – and others are intensely private. Some are very funny, satirical, or sardonic; some are serious or somber; some are deeply personal and some are deeply political and public (plate 4 shows two of Milton's sonnets in his own handwriting).

There is no way to pin Milton down to one type of subject matter or tone or color that should be used in sonnets. Almost none of the sonnets are about the conventional or customary topic of the Renaissance sonnet cycle, love, and not one of them is concerned with the kind of jealous love triangle that Shakespeare celebrates in his sonnets. In fact, Milton's sonnets have almost nothing to do with the poetic style or substance of Shakespeare's sonnets: where Shakespeare's sonnets are homely, Milton's avoid household or barnyard imagery; where Shakespeare might take on such as serious subject as lust, Milton disdains the subject; where Shakespeare encourages a young friend to marry, Milton focuses on love within marriage. Milton's concerns are conditioned by Puritan views toward love within the domestic sphere, toward politics as they reflect the responsibility of the individual god-fearing individual, even toward friendship as a Christian duty. His sonnets can be more intimate than Shakespeare's at times, less abstract than Sidney's or Spenser's love sonnets written to unobtainable and capricious women.

The most intimate of the sonnets, such as "Methought I saw my late espoused saint" or "When I consider how my light is spent," are deeply personal, concerned with the eternal problems of mortality and the waste of time as the potential waste of a life God has given someone like Milton to accomplish great things. But not one is concerned with the earthly immortality conferred by poetic art, as are many of Shakespeare's sonnets.

The occasionally lustful tone of the often frustrated love sonnets of Sidney, Spenser, or Shakespeare is quickly discarded in favor of a kind of Puritan respect for intelligent and courageous women, and deep and permanent conjugal love. One can observe Milton outgrowing what he called "vain amatorious poetry" (as with the love poetry of Shakespeare or the seductive poetry of Ovid's *Elegies*) within the variety of his sonnets. Typically, Milton in his collected printed poetry allows the reader to see him in the process of maturing as a poet, from vaguely erotic juvenilia in Italian eventually to one quiet, serious sonnet in which the apparition of his dead wife is compared with the tragic figure of Alcestis, risen from the dead. In the sonnet to his dead wife, Milton stretches the nutshell of the sonnet form to fit the scope of a tragic play.

Though editions of Milton's sonnets have been compiled by J. S. Smart and E. A. J. Honigmann, and they have been examined closely in an admirable book by Anna Nardo, the sonnets remain resistant to being treated as unified by theme or poetic form. Milton is a great sonnet-writer, the critics agree, and he is called the last of the great English sonnet-writers before Romantic poets such as Wordsworth took up the form again, but he is typically unpredictable and he resists fitting anyone's definition of the sonneteer, especially because he never uses traditional Petrarchan imagery and he never, in English, celebrates love before marriage.

Arcades and *A Masque* (known as *Comus*)

In 1634, Milton apparently accepted a paid commission from John Egerton, the Earl of Bridgewater, one of His Majesty's Privy Council members and the incipient Lord President of Wales, to write a masque that would celebrate the installation of the Earl as Lord President in his castle in Ludlow. It may be better to follow Cedric Brown's name for what Milton wrote, "aristocratic entertainment," but Milton was consciously or unconsciously cagey or dodgy about his title: he used the generic *A Masque*, and qualified that only by calling his work a masque at Ludlow. Later editors were the ones to begin labeling his masque, somewhat perversely, after its chief villain, as *Comus*.

We do not know for sure if money changed hands, whether the Earl provided an income for Milton as he wrote the masque, and we don't even know if Milton ever went to Ludlow to see his masque rehearsed or performed. There is no sure evidence in the masque itself to tell us where it was performed, or whether it was performed indoors or out. We do know that Milton had already written *Arcades*, a pastoral musical entertainment, a kind of mini-masque, for Alice Spencer Egerton, Dowager Countess of Derby, who was John Egerton's mother-in-law and stepmother at the same time.

By the time Milton accepted her patronage, the Dowager Countess of Derby was a grande dame of literary England. Her deceased first husband, Ferdinando Stanley, Lord Strange and later Earl of Derby, had supported Edmund Spenser, who celebrated him as "Amyntas" in *Colin Clout's Come Home Again*, and had for a time been sponsor of an acting company in which Shakespeare had performed. Because one of his titles was "King" of the Isle of Man, Milton could call his wife a "rural Queen" (108) in *Arcades*. Her second husband was Sir Thomas Egerton, Lord Chancellor Ellesmere, to whom John Donne was secretary, and she is known to have danced as a young woman in masques written by Ben Jonson. As William Hunter puts it, "Who else can claim direct relationships with Spenser, Shakespeare, Jonson, Donne, and Milton?" (*Family Piece* 15).

Arcades is an elaborate compliment to the Dowager Countess, set at her country estate, Harefield, for performance in good weather out of doors, with the alternative of an indoor venue (Brown 51). The name has little to do with the modern meaning of arcade as "amusement park": it can be translated as "The Arcadians," since it celebrates people supposed to be living in Arcady, the most famous pastoral setting of ancient Greek poetry. *Arcades* (pronounce it Ár-ca-des) is a musical entertainment, probably employing the talents of the composer Henry Lawes, a royal court musician also in service to the Egerton family as music-teacher to the Earl of Bridgewater's children. Henry Lawes's brother William may also have been involved. William had written music for the London theater, specifically for the King's Men. We know that William and Henry Lawes had visited Harefield in 1634, if not before (Brown 13).

Dating *Arcades* is difficult: Hunter places it in 1634, about four months before Milton's more famous masque was produced in Ludlow, but other biographers and editors have dated it as early as 1632. It is closely related to Milton's more ambitious masque, being concerned with the conflict between good and evil in a pastoral setting, with a "Genius of the Wood" instead of an "Attendant Spirit" as master of ceremonies. The role of Henry Lawes within one character or the other would hardly have changed from Lady Alice Spencer's estate to Ludlow Castle. The tissues of allusions and layers of pastoral names are also very close to those of the masque and of "L'Allegro" and "Il Penseroso."

The entertainment honors Lady Alice Spencer, flatters her, and places her among the Arcadians partly because of where she lives, among rolling hills, gardens, avenues of elms, away from the city, at Harefield in Middlesex. In her youth, Alice Spencer had been celebrated as lavishly as had Queen Elizabeth. Milton was probably aware that Harefield, in the person of Lady Alice and her then husband Sir Thomas Egerton, honored Queen Elizabeth in 1602 with an aristocratic entertainment including a text by Sir John Davies (Brown 16).

Milton was, then, probably collaborating with the musicians Henry and William Lawes in service to a noble lady, relating himself poetically and through Lady Alice's patronage to Edmund Spenser (the Countess's distant relative), Sir Thomas Davies, Ben Jonson, William Shakespeare (through the Earl of Derby's support for his company), John Donne (through Sir Thomas Egerton), and even John Marston, who had in 1607 provided an entertainment in her honor (Brown 16).

Arcades is both occasional and topical through its associations with the Countess and Harefield, and it is made universal through its pastoral setting and promotion of universal harmony. Though a modern reader might devalue it as gross flattery, about underlings kissing the hem of a garment of an aristocrat (see line 83, for instance), it is also about the power of music, it is beautiful lyric and dramatic poetry, and it has the freshness of imagery of "Lycidas" and of "L'Allegro" and "Il Penseroso."

Milton's full-scale aristocratic entertainment, generically named as *A Masque* (the spellings "mask" and "masque" were variants of the same word in English, though the dramatic form was Italian, as in Giuseppe Verdi's opera *Un Ballo in maschera* – a masked ball) is similar in theme, allusion, poetic devices, lyricism, to Milton's earlier aristocratic entertainment, but it is not flattery for a single aristocrat as was *Arcades*. Instead, it praises the bearing and the good taste of the entire family of the Lord President of Wales. Thomas Egerton was also Earl of Bridgewater and a member of King Charles I's Privy Council, a very powerful and wealthy man.

It is also difficult for a modern reader to imagine the importance of the Bridgewater–Egerton–Spencer family grouping to the literature of Milton's generation. The various Bridgewater and Ellesmere collections of books and manuscripts, for instance, have formed the core of some of the great libraries of England and America, including the Huntington Library in California. Milton's position, considering the importance of the first Earl of Bridgewater, seems to have been one of respect without toadyism. Neither *Arcades* nor *A Masque* are quite like the average frothy, flattering masque of the early seventeenth century. The aristocratic children performing in Milton's masque, for instance, are not in the traditional masks that gave the genre its name but that disguise the identity of the performer, allowing the actors to hide behind the masks. Why do the performers in Milton's conception of masque need to be masked? They are not hiding anything, nor are they deceiving the audience. The good children of Milton's masques are protected by their natural aristocratic bearing and their intelligence. Distorted disguises are saved for the evil Comus and his deceived rout of half-animal followers, labeled "oughly-headed Monsters" (the ugly-headed monsters of line 695).

Evil needs to wear a mask, and even the masks of evil are ugly because evil itself is ugly. Comus will take on the disguise of a simple cottager, but even that disguise will be quickly revealed to be a fraud. Good people need no masks, and evil is quickly unmasked.

The pretense of Milton's masque is that England is the true Arcadia, as compared to the Greek one, and that the Attendant Spirit who serves the Earl of Bridgewater is in touch with Jove and other divinities through the divine medium of music. We are in a Platonic world in which an ideal sphere exists outside the human: the Attendant Spirit flies between the real and the ideal world. The most perfect of mortals, the Lady, can hear the music of the spheres, the divine harmonies of the universe. The name of the Attendant Spirit, also called the Dæmon in the Greek sense of "daimon" or spirit with divine power, raises the Earl's music-master and Milton's friend Henry Lawes to the status of a heroic composer in touch with divine harmony. He should in no way be thought of as a "demon," since that would reduce him to the status of fallen angel rather than Greek demigod.

The Attendant Spirit is also a "genius of the shore" like Edward King in "Lycidas" or a "Genius of the Wood" like the one mentioned in "Il Penseroso," a tutelary spirit in charge of a region: Henry Lawes is made into a spirit keeping divine order in a specific region of England, the border with Wales. He resembles the pagan equivalent, but being English and Christian makes him a more respectable kind of genie or *genius loci*.

Musical entertainment

Milton's masque is a musical entertainment, the private and aristocratic version of a Broadway musical, costing as much or as little as the aristocratic family wanted to spend. Milton's collaborator was the musically gifted Henry Lawes, Charles I's music-master but also famous among poets for preserving the sense of their words within the vocal line. The songs in the masque are remarkably easy to understand – even with a modern audience not used to the vocabulary – when the singers enunciate well. Lawes and Milton are not exactly the seventeenth-century equivalent of Lerner and Loewe or Rogers and Hammerstein, but they did work well together.

Milton's compliment to Lawes in a complementary sonnet is that he "First taught our English Musick how to span / Words with just note and accent . . ." (*Riverside* 252). In other words, Lawes's chief claim to fame was matching English music with English poetry. The cosmic myth of the music of the spheres is reinforced by the harmony between words and music. The Attendant Spirit (not forgetting that he is also Henry Lawes) is in touch not only with the domain of the Earl of Bridgewater, but he can also hear and emulate the music of the spheres. He can also write music easy for Alice Bridgewater to sing and Milton can write words easy for the audience to understand. That doesn't mean that Milton's words are simple or his musical entertainment simplistic or simple-minded. The music of the spheres was always a serious business for him, a junction between God and human beings.

Music in the masque form is a two-edged sword that can fight for good or for evil. Any music associated with Comus as conjurer and necromancer, as with dances performed by monsters, would have to be seductive, loose, overly sensuous, demonic music. In the text the dances are described merely as "the measure," and we have to assume that Henry or William Lawes wrote devilish music, music that has not survived, for the monsters to dance to. (For an equivalent, listen to the music associated with the underworld and Cerberus in Gluck's famous opera, *Orfeo ed Euridice*, as in the London Philharmonic Orchestra CD conducted by Jane Glover and Raymond Leppard, Erato 5864). The music that has survived is for the songs set by Henry Lawes, music on the side of good, as with the Lady's song to Echo, and Sabrina's song of white magic conjuration that helps to break the spell on the Lady. Stephen Buehler has recently demonstrated the magical force of musical mathematics, creating something like ecstasy in the singer and the sung-to, according to Renaissance theories of the power of music, as set forth by Galileo's father Vincenzo Galilei. Music, like wine, could be used well for its deliciousness or misused for its ability to induce drunken behavior.

We are also within a Christian world in which Jove can be the same as the Christian God and in which the negative Dionysian spirit of dissolute revelry is discordant and evil. The very name of Milton's antagonist is derived from the Greek word for banquet or drunken party out of control, transliterated as *komos*, which of course is personified in the demi-god named Comus, who has the power to render his victims comatose. In the very name of Comus, Milton cleverly combines traditions ranging from the New Testament listing of "lasciviousness, lusts, excess of wine, revellings, banquettings, and abominable idolatories" (1 Peter 4:3–4; see Brown 69–70). Following Comus is more than just comestibles or good food. The banquet Comus offers prefigures the temptation of food to Christ in the wilderness, one of the temptations Milton examines in *Paradise Regain'd*.

Milton's masque is also a variant on the folk tale of the babes in the wood, as in the tale of Hansel and Gretel threatened by the witch or the Goose Girl who temporarily loses her identity as a princess. The children lost in the wood outside Ludlow are not under threat of being eaten by a witch or of being treated like peasants, but they are under attack by a powerful sorcerer, a son of Circe, and that sorcerer would like to make the Lady his bride. Scholars have suggested that the situation in the masque might be based on a real-life rape trial in which the Earl of Bridgewater was the judge (Marcus). With potential for rape in the woods (meeting wicked witches or sorcerers is bad enough), and with Comus's brag that he would like to make the Lady his "queen," the masque takes on a very sinister undertone, and the threat to the 15-year-old Lady's virginity becomes horrifying. Even the apparently innocent image of the Lady as nightingale points to the possible comparison between the Lady and Philomela in Ovid's *Metamorphoses*, who is raped and mutilated. Some modern critics I have talked to find the masque "creepy." The image of the nightingale used by the Lady in her song, "Sweet Echo" (it begins at line 230) does recall the horrible fate of Philomela in Ovid's tale of rape and dismemberment, which became the central myth of Shakespeare's *Titus Andronicus*. And Echo is not just the pleasant if mysterious acoustic phenomenon associated with caves or valleys; it is the name of Ovid's nymph who pined herself to death through her own unhealthy worship of the self-loving Narcissus.

Members of the Bridgewater family very close to the Earl were also involved in a heavily publicized scandal in 1631 that ran the family name through the muck of depraved behavior, including rape, sodomy, and voyeurism. Mervyn Touchet, the Earl of Castlehaven, second husband of the Countess of Derby's daughter Anne, forced his wife and servants of both sexes to perform various perverse acts in front of him, acts that were at the time punishable by death. The Earl and several of his servants were indeed executed for their crimes. The case put a large stain on the escutcheon of the Bridgewater family.

To Milton's credit, he does not seem to allude to the scandal at all, but lines that were perhaps cut by a "censor" (Brown 173) in which the Lady alludes to "likerish [lecherous] baits fit to ensnare a brute" do imply that Comus would like to tempt the Lady to lechery, and all the references in the masque to chastity or virginity – whether they represent Lady Alice Egerton's present physical state, her innocence, or her moral perfection – seem to skate close to the edge of bad taste and to the violation of social decorum. Lady Alice Egerton was of marriageable age, and, given the moral strictures of her time, her chastity would have been assumed or taken for granted, but certainly it would not often have been a topic for public discussion. Milton's presentation of Lady Alice's chastity, which provokes laughter in a jaded audience whenever the word "Chastity" is mentioned, might have annoyed the patriarch Bridgewater and his wife when the masque was performed for them, despite the obvious moral strength of the Lady and the elegance of her lines.

The masque's plot and performance

The plot is simple: the three Bridgewater children – Lady Alice Egerton being the oldest at 15 – become separated from each other in a sinister wood near their father's castle, with the sister ending up alone, exposing the young virgin to potential harm. The Attendant Spirit (never forgetting that he is also the children's music tutor Henry Lawes) attempts to protect the Lady, both in his normal costume and when he poses as a shepherd, and her two brothers attempt to act manfully in her defense. The Lady, however, being armed with her own virtue, is stronger than she might seem and needs no protection. Even against the charms of a vile and deceptive sorcerer and conjurer who can deceive her eyes by taking on the shape of a simple peasant, she has the strengths of chastity, truth, nobility, and reason on her side. She is certainly willing and able to "just say no."

The two boys, being boys, are more careless than the Lady, their big sister, who is abandoned rather than getting lost on her own (they lose her; she doesn't lose them). The boys practice typical chivalric carelessness of men losing women or allowing them to get lost, and then hunting for them. The Attendant Spirit cannot save the Lady on his own, because of his lower rank: she has to do it by resisting Comus's fallacious logic, and Sabrina is an appropriate sister to help her, even if the Attendant Spirit instigates the union. The social markers in the masque show Comus as of a rank contemptible to the Bridgewaters: he is of a different caste, being a disreputable Greek-derived Ludlow wood-sprite son of a witch (Circe). The Lady should not even have to talk to him, after she discovers that he is not one of her father's shepherds, because he is a contemptible, animalistic brute – like one of his own ugly-headed beasts, morally speaking.

When he is chased away by the boys, he slinks off, defeated by the Lady's holy chastity, just as Satan in the Serpent slinks off in *Paradise Lost*, except that Satan has scored a temporary victory with Eve and Comus hasn't scored at all. The truism from *Samson Agonistes* that "all wickedness is weakness," by foresight or hindsight, operates in the masque.

By hindsight, the modern reader of Milton's masque can see the temptations of *Paradise Lost*, *Samson Agonistes*, and *Paradise Regain'd* built into it. The Lady is like Eve on the one hand (an Eve who does not give in to temptation) and like the Son of God of *Paradise Regain'd* on the other, eloquent in her debate against the subtle evil of a powerful tempter. Samson has at times fallen for the sensual temptations and lies of a Comus or Dalila, but in the end, like the Lady, he resists falling for evil.

To give Milton's rhetorical art full credit, Comus argues from the powerful position of praising the abundance of nature. The Lady's beauty is only natural, she should celebrate it, joy in it, and allow him to worship her as if she were a goddess. Comus at times sounds like Andrew Marvell's potential lover asking his coy mistress to go to bed with him. Instead of being seduced, the Lady sees through his deceptive offer of pleasure without moral worth, and she defeats the Satanic Comus even though he immobilizes her by creating a magical bond between her and the chair she sits in, cementing her to the chair. With what is often comic pedantry, scholars have been arguing for years exactly what bonding agent Comus uses to make her stick to the chair! She is, however, immobile only long enough to be rescued by a local river goddess, Sabrina, who herself has escaped male violence and has been given white magic powers to release virgins from any spells cast on them.

Interestingly enough, the Bridgewater children had complained of demonic possession and had been treated, not long before the masque was produced, by the noted physician John Napier (Breasted, "Another Bewitching"). Napier's medical methods, which included the manufacture of protective amulets and the use of St. John's wort, are instructive for showing a modern reader the connections between seventeenth-century magic, the equivalent of psychiatry, and medicine. The masque can be viewed as the unspelling of Lady Alice, but that would be too simplistic an interpretation, because the forces urging the Lady to resist evil are larger than any local contest between physician and mentally troubled patient.

Politics

The politics of Milton's masque may undermine its genre. The Lady, played by the daughter of a member of His Majesty's Privy Council, is made to say that courtesy itself, which should derive from courts,

> oft is sooner found in lowly sheds
> With smoaky rafters, then in tapstry Halls
> And Courts of Princes, where it first was nam'd,
> And yet is most pretended.
>
> (ll. 323–6)

Her comment on princely courts and tapestried halls seems to be subversive, on the part of the incipient Puritan author. He seems to be undercutting the very social class – that of the Earl of Bridgewater – which has paid the bills for the production of his masque. To at least one author of a monograph on the subject, the modern reader should think of it as *Milton's Puritan Masque* (McGuire). The poet would later to be able to dismiss the entire genre as part of a group of dissolute aristocratic social events – "Court Amours, / Mixt Dance, or wanton Mask, or Midnight Bal" – in *Paradise Lost* (4.767–8). Milton's masque has in its social structure, perhaps, the seeds of its own destruction, and it may be, in Stanley Fish's provoking phrase, "a self-consuming artifact."

Comus's language is rich, allusive, beautiful, exotic – like Oberon's speeches in Shakespeare's *Midsummer Night's Dream* – but he is no match for the power of the Lady's mind. The Lady, despite the fact that she is acted by a 15-year-old, is a great debater, as wise as Socrates as depicted in a Platonic dialogue, as formidable as Spenser's warrior princess Britomart, and as resistant to evil as Isabella in *Measure for Measure*. Her voice is the voice of pure reason, unadorned. She needs no glitz, no glitter; she needs no hollow rhetoric to conquer the evil beauty of Comus's temptations.

The Lady is saved, partly by the strength of her own mind and partly by a *dea ex machina*. The spell that glued her to the chair is broken by Sabrina, the nymph associated with the river Severn, which flows near Ludlow. One older school of English pronunciation pronounces her name "Sah-brine-ah," emphasizing the salinity or brininess of a tidal river like the Severn. Sabrina is a product of the mythologizing of British history: like any of Ovid's transformed nymphs in the *Metamorphoses*, she has become what she is at the time presented in the masque through a change of one life form into another. She is a woman who once, under threat of rape, was transformed into something like a river goddess who attends forever after to the needs of threatened virgins such as the Lady. She is, in other words, like any number of Ovidian nymphs who avoided rape by metamorphosis.

The Lady, as her powerful generic name suggests, needs no human limitation because she is something like a force of aristocratic nature. She is also more than Lady Alice Egerton. She may not be Lady Alice any more than the Attendant Spirit need be Henry Lawes, because each character is representative of something like an allegorical truth. The Lady is Chastity personified, but she is more than a name like "Chastity" would imply. She is the one just woman who has the inherent power to resist evil in the form of Comus's temptations, one on one, alone against a powerful oppressor.

Performances of the masque vary considerably. Here is a review I wrote of a staging at the Folger Shakespeare Library, Washington, in March of 2001:

> Any one review of the performance of the masque at the Folger would probably disagree with all others, about actors, dancers, musicians, costumes, lighting, choreography. Most of the members of the audience, I am sure, were just glad to have an opportunity to see a performance of a work so rarely performed.
>
> A director has several important choices: should Comus be played as a young Bacchus, dripping odors, dripping wine, with curly locks, or should he be a dirty old man, unctuous or slimy? Traditionally, anyone kin to Bacchus should be a belly-god, and Stephen Orgel

showed the one prior English (Inigo Jones) Comus as a fat naked Bacchus-type.

The Folger director, Richard Clifford, casting himself in the role of Comus, had to present a slender, suave, middle-aged Comus, inclining toward the slimy rather than the overweight.

Another important choice is whether to present the principal actors as static, operatic characters at lecterns, or whether to make them memorize their lines and move about the stage. Because of thrift, the Folger actors read their lines from the lecterns: they weren't off-book yet. This choice means the difference between a Broadway musical masque and an oratorio in which the actors say or sing their lines from one fixed position.

The reviewer from the *Washington Post* called the performance a Milton soap-opera, which was unkind, but he did commend the clear reading of the lines (this was amazing: from the rear of the Folger theater, the famous reconstruction of the Globe, I could hear every word); the music of Henry Lawes and others played by the highly professional Folger Consort led by Robert Eisenstein; and the period dancing choreographed by Julie Andrijeski. The singing was one-third professional (Sabrina, as sung by Rosa Lamoreaux), and two-thirds proficient (everyone else hit the notes on schedule).

I was a jaded viewer, having seen the work performed so often in the last thirty years, so my opinion of what Comus should look like, or what movement is necessary, or what color or texture the costumes should be, was also jaded.

As with any performed art based on words on a page, Milton's masque can be changed considerably from one performance to the next. If the costuming is modern, for instance, the audience may see the cosmic drama in timeless terms, rather than seeing Botticelli women in gauzy gowns and men in tights. If the Lady is indeed 15, as was Lady Alice Egerton, her virginity does indeed need to be protected against any masher like Comus. If the two boy players are sub-teens, their Platonic dialogue takes on a quaintness that lines spoken by mature young men would not have. And if Comus is a dirty old man, he is quite different from a young Bacchic degenerate.

Even the singing will alter the effect of performances, as when an opera singer takes on a major role in a Broadway musical. It may be appropriate for the actor who plays Sabrina to be professionally trained, but, if she is, the untrained voice of the Lady might be shown up to be amateurish if a professional sings Sabrina. Ideally,

the Attendant Spirit should be a professional actor and singer, the
Lady a very well-trained amateur, and the Sabrina the best local
soprano available, but all actors need to be able to speak Milton's
sophisticated lines with admirable pacing, breath control, and emphasis, in order not to produce laughter in the wrong places. An
actor might even have to de-emphasize the word "chastity" in order
not to get a laugh (after the director has decided whether or not the
line deserves to be laughed at).

Early in Milton's prose and poetry, a keen reader begins to observe the emergence of the individual human being as a force for
change, for self-knowledge, for a moral center, as with the Lady in
the masque. Milton's Adam, or his individual "master spirit" who
produces a book as his own "pretious life-blood" (*Riverside* 999), is a
unique individual who can write a book that the world will not
allow to disappear. The reader of a masterwork like *Areopagitica* can
see that Milton's vital prose embodies a master spirit who is himself
crying out to his readership "Do not let my work die." Milton's effort on behalf of the individual, though at times elitist and sometimes self-centered, also represents a faith in human intellect and
will. Milton is always open to charges of egocentrism or deep intellectual snobbishness, but he can always be seen as "himself a true
poem," a good man in quest of universal truth in his art.

Censorship, Milton realizes, can kill the human spirit, just as the
imprimaturs of Roman Catholic censors stifled the spirit of the authors contained within the pages they censored. Milton's lonely fight
against pre-publication censorship, in this case by what he considered to be limited bureaucrats, is echoed in his fight for domestic
liberty in the divorce tracts and his less lonely fight against the power
of the bishops in his antiprelatical tracts.

The Prose Tracts

Beginning with *Of Reformation* in 1641, Milton began the work of
reforming what now is called the Church of England, the Anglican
Church, or the Protestant Episcopal Church. He saw the great evil of
the church in its episcopal hierarchy, its rule by bishops. Bishops
were appointed through the power of the king, for a lifetime tenure.
They were wealthy men – always men, and never women – who

often lived in palaces. Matters of the spirit were neglected. Ceremony and vestments were all that mattered in church, style was more important than substance, ministry to the people was ignored. The bishop or archbishop represented temporal power because he could designate which of the graduates of Oxford or Cambridge might receive benefices or church livings.

Milton would have preferred that bishops be elected from within the church, "by the hands of the whole *Church*" (*Riverside* 880), not appointed by the king. Just as the king should be the servant of the people, the ruler of the church should be a benevolent servant of his parishioners.

Milton was hardly alone in his battle against the corruption of the English church. In the Elizabethan era, anonymous pamphleteers wrote what were corporately known as the "Marprelate" tracts. Taking their name from the marring or defaming of prelates (plus perhaps a touch of Martin Luther, since the author of some of the tracts was identified as "Martin Marprelate"), they recommended reform of the church from the inside and they used scornful laughter as a weapon against their political adversaries (Corns, *Uncloistered Virtue* 204). Milton's antiprelatical tracts raised the level of discourse, rarely slinging mud or insulting his adversaries – which techniques he saved for his later attacks on political opponents Salmasius and Alexander More.

Of Reformation battles against what Milton calls "outward conformity" (*Riverside* 876), the meaningless ceremony, costume, and ritual of what he considered the corrupt church. Meanwhile the bishops, according to Milton, were ignoring the parishioners in order to say "Make us rich, make us lofty, make us lawlesse" (*Riverside* 884). In order to deflate the notion of rich bishops and meaningless rituals, Milton translates passages of poetry from Dante, Petrarch, and Ariosto that speak against the Emperor Constantine's effort to give the church temporal power and wealth (*Riverside* 884). In other words, Milton used the strength of his right hand – his poetic abilities – in service to what he called the left-hand effort of his prose.

The Reason of Church Government (1642)

Milton's second antiprelatical tract is noteworthy to literary critics and biographers more than to church historians in that it includes a

large chunk of autobiography in its second book. The biographical
segment seems to come out of nowhere, since it has little to do with
church government and everything to do with Milton, the young
man of conscience and the fledgling poet, contributing "those few
talents which God at that present had lent me" (*Riverside* 921) to a
cause in which he believed. He talks about being a fledgling scholar
inside "the full circle of [his] private studies" (922) forced out of
silence by the religious cause of reforming the church, when he would
much rather be "a Poet soaring in the high region of his fancies with
his garland and singing robes about him" (922). Milton pictures himself as he was honored by the fellowship of scholars and poets in
Italy, again irrelevant to his subject matter, and he talks about his
own ambition to rival Homer, Vergil, and Tasso in epic writing, or
Sophocles or Euripides in writing tragedy, or Pindar and Callimachus
in writing odes and hymns. This has little to do with church government, which Milton drags back in at the end of the pamphlet, when
he pictures himself "comming to some maturity of years and
perceaving what tyranny had invaded the Church," because he had
been "Church-outed by the Prelats" (925); therefore, he had to write
of the reason of church government. One can hear, in the association
between "tyranny" and "Church," a lifelong and constant resistance
in Milton's personality and in his public career to unjust authority,
whether it was in the home (a drunken husband or unfaithful wife),
in the state (a tyrannical king), or in the church (prelates command-
ing parishioners to come to church or bow to the image of the cross).

   The years 1643 and 1644 were extraordinary for the still-young
poet and potential public servant who had finished his formal education and his private period of reading, had been to continental
Europe, had gotten married and had been deserted, and had become involved in the politics of revolution. The year 1645 would
also mark his emergence into the world of the published poet, with
his name on the title page (plate 5). Milton must have been juggling
poetry manuscripts, divorce tracts, antiprelatical diatribes, and
Areopagitica in reaction to his divorce tracts being censored and publicly condemned in Parliament.

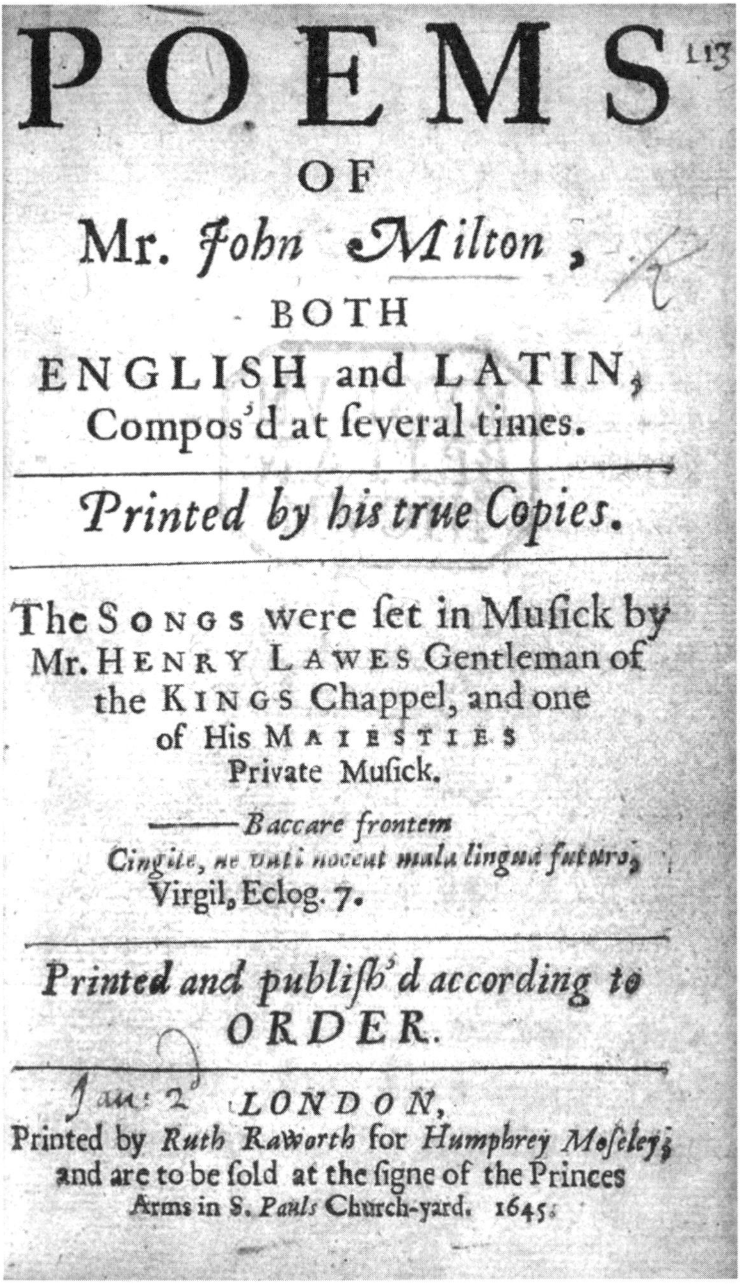

POEMS

OF

Mr. *John Milton*,

·BOTH

ENGLISH and LATIN,

Compos'd at several times.

Printed by his true Copies.

The SONGS were set in Musick by
Mr. HENRY LAWES Gentleman of
the KINGS Chappel, and one
of His MAIESTIES
Private Musick.

————*Baccare frontem*
Cingite, ne vati noceat mala lingua futuro,
Virgil, Eclog. 7.

Printed and publish'd according to
ORDER.

Jan: 2 LONDON,
Printed by *Ruth Raworth* for *Humphrey Moseley*,
and are to be sold at the signe of the Princes
Arms in S. *Pauls* Church-yard. 1645.

Plate 5   The title page of Milton's 1645 *Poems*. © British Library, London.

Of Education

Milton fought another isolated battle for a reform, this time in the English educational system, in his small tract *Of Education*, published in one of his wonder years, 1644. In the open public arena of the pamphleteers projecting an ideal commonwealth in the 1640s, "pamphlets were eight or sixteen pages long, long enough to argue a single point" (Achinstein 10). Milton's pamphlet was not typical in that it was not exclusively topical. He would like to make his scheme timeless, a universal scheme for improving all education at any point in history, even if his suggestions for improving education were based on his small-scale experience in educating the sons of relatives and of aristocrats he knew. *Of Education* does not refer extensively to other pamphlets on the subject, and it is remarkably original and personal, being based on Milton's own schooling and on his practical experience as tutor and headmaster.

Milton thought enough of the eight-page essay to include it with the 1673 reissue of his poems, but it may have originally been intended for a coterie readership, that of the scientific and educational speculators or projectors centered around the reformer Samuel Hartlib. Milton addressed the tract to Hartlib, who privately acknowledged Milton as having "written many good books[;] a great traveller and full of p[ro]iects and inventions" (French, *Life Records* 2.82).

Of Education is a reformer's list of suggestions about how to improve pre-college and college education in England. Milton's scheme would allow an educational system in England to provide students of ages of about 10 to 20 with a version of his own education, largely at public expense. As usual when he is arguing on paper, Milton is proud of his own ideas and puts them forward with confidence. He is typically disdainful of customary education in places like Cambridge, which had been too much governed by what Milton called "the Scholastick grosnesse of barbarous ages" (*Riverside* 981). He even disagrees with some of the theories of John Amos Comenius, whose career in England Samuel Hartlib had sponsored. But his system of education seems today to be humane and even enjoyable, if very rigorous. Schoolboys should begin work at 6 or 7 a.m. and go on until early evening, with breaks for exercising and eating. The children should be instructed how to master Latin and Greek in a very short time, in about one year, but they should master the language while reading history and literature at least partly for pleasure. Education at times should be a game, and it should be fun. Classical comedies were part of the curriculum, and Milton, despite being strict, was also reported to be jolly and convivial with his students. According to more than one of his pupils, he was never pedantic. His instruction was charitable or generous as well, and it extended to his family and friends. Milton "opened" difficult passages that his friend and pupil Thomas Ellwood was reading to him after Milton had gone blind. And his daughter Deborah was instructed in some of the languages that her father had her read to him, to the extent that she became a schoolmistress in later life. Milton stayed in touch with his former pupils, keeping them not as "contacts" in the aristocratic world he was on the outskirts of but as friends, as with "Lawrence of virtuous father," celebrated by Milton in a friendly sonnet, and Edward Phillips, and Thomas Ellwood. Milton's other nephew pupil, John Phillips, was to write sometimes scurrilous, scatological, and obscene verse in the manner of the Roman poet Martial, satirizing Puritan hypocrisy. His uncle might have approved of satire targeting hypocrisy. Phillips's *Sportive Wit*, published in 1656, was ordered burnt by the Council of State and the order to burn it was approved by Oliver Cromwell (Campbell 165–6), but Milton never himself descended into obscene satire, at least not in verse. It is hard to tell whose side Milton would have been on when an offensive work by his own nephew was burned, but there is evidence that John Phillips sided with the monarchy and turned against his uncle, politically at least. In 1685, in a long and prolific writing career that in many ways is a lower-echelon imitation of his uncle's literary effort, he published *An Humble Offering to the Sacred Memory of . . . Charles II*.

Milton had a strong dislike for useless learning. Though his scheme may have been limited to the children of nobility, it was practical, and it included study units devoted to agricultural land use, shepherding, hunting, and fishing. Geography instruction included the use of globes. Music instruction included singing and the playing of instruments. Military instruction included marching and sweaty exercise with a weapon. Education may have practical value in training citizens to make their country better through scientific experimentation – the best way to plow land efficiently, for instance, or the best ways to raise bees for honey and wax. Sundays at Milton's projected school might be spent, quite naturally for the holy day, reading Scripture and studying theology (Milton does not mention church-going, and he might have come to believe in something like religious home-schooling). Logic and rhetoric were not to be taught in a void: they were to be taught by the example lived by the school-master – in this case an instructor who never stopped writing argumentatively throughout his whole career. Milton's educational scheme included what modern educators would call "service-learning," or at least it included a component of practical field work, if not public service. Though Milton's students never built houses for the poor that we know of, they at least conducted some of their research in the real world where real people raised bees or practiced military formations in preparation for war.

The divorce debate

The divorce tracts began with *The Doctrine and Discipline of Divorce*, the first edition of which was published in August 1643. That little book was immediately misunderstood, as far as Milton could see, and he published a much revised and augmented edition in February of 1644, to be followed by *Tetrachordon* and *Colasterion* in 1645. (By 1645 the Civil War was heating up; Milton was reconciled to his wife; and in 1646 her whole family moved in with their son-in-law.) The divorce tracts were a political outrage, a personal scandal, and an affront to the sacrament of marriage as it had been understood by the Church of England. Nevertheless, Milton wrote them, and their prose is almost as energetic as that of *Areopagitica*, even if the cause of divorce must be more tenuously argued. Milton was arguing with his in-laws, with the church, with the state, and with public opinion. He had on his side very few proponents of divorce or of an even more outrageous practice, patriarchal bigamy or polygamy.

From our vantage point looking back from the twenty-first century, Milton's legal and spiritual arguments are fascinating to read as cultural history – if they are read by the light of the laws of any country that permits legal and religious divorce. They are prophetic in that Milton argues that divorce should be allowed to exist by law and by religious permission. Vicious incompatibility is an unholy state for a husband and wife to be yoked together in. Dylan Thomas's memorable phrase, "bound in hold bedlock," comes mischievously to mind. Sex, which should be beautiful and creative in a good marriage, is in a bad marriage ugly and abhorrent: it is "to grind in the mill of an undelighted and servil copulation" (*Doctrine and Discipline of Divorce; Riverside* 942). Milton's rich but disgusting image for enforced sexual slavery within a loveless marriage – as a Samson-like slave bondage – sticks in the mind and in the craw of the reader. It does also look forward to the Samson of *Samson Agonistes*, attempting to escape the bonds of marriage to his betrayer Dalila. Milton's dramatic character, unlike the biblical Samson, is married to Dalila and therefore needs a divorce from a political and religious traitor. Milton has a way of tying all his most passionately felt causes together in his imagery, and images in his divorce tracts are echoed in *Paradise Lost* and in *Samson Agonistes*.

Areopagitica: the prose masterpiece

Milton's prose is often studied for itself, even though it is political, topical, and sometimes mean-spirited in the heat of argument. Milton wrote against the power of the English bishops (his tracts are called antiprelatical because church officials were called "prelates"), for the institution of divorce 300 years before it became law, for the liberty of the press for unlicenced printing 100 years before it became the law in the American colonies, and for the liberty of the people to depose and even try and execute a monarch (so much for the divine right of kings). He also proposed a reformed educational system for England; he wrote grammars, dictionaries, and rhetorics to aid his countrymen with learning their own language and other languages such as Greek and Latin; and he apparently compiled not only a now-lost theological index but a full and systematic Christian doctrine in an attempt to strengthen his own faith.

In all his prose writing, he was rarely anonymous; he was more like a self-proclaimed intellectual giant, a kind of Samson showing off his own force of argument or a kind of Solomon spreading the wisdom of his deep reading. In his prose, he never forgets he is first a poet. He writes prose only (he himself said) as if he were writing with his left hand, yet his richest prose, as in *Areopagitica*, is as rich as poetry. It deserves to be read aloud. Here is a famous passage describing England as a kind of phoenix or as a St. Paul on the road to Emmaus, with scales falling from his eyes:

> Methinks I see her as an Eagle muing her mighty youth, and kindling
> her undazl'd eyes at the full midday beam; purging and unscaling her
> long abused sight at the fountain it self of heav'nly radiance; while
> the whole noise of timorous and flocking birds, with those also that
> love the twilight, flutter about, amaz'd at what she means, and in
> their envious gabble would prognosticat a year of sects and schisms.
> (*Riverside* 1000)

Milton's prose is so rich, so full of images, and so allusive here that
poems can be made out of it. The Eagle becomes an emblem of the
adventurous state emerging into maturity, looking with eagle eyes
straight into the sun, into heavenly radiance, while the small flock-
ing birds symbolize useless or foolish citizens, fluttering aimlessly
and wasting motion in envy and meaningless talk of sects and
schisms. All of *Areopagitica* is like that: too rich and exciting and
meaningful to be classified as ordinary prose.

Adam is in *Areopagitica* as well, exemplifying free will and the decision to pursue good or evil. Adam and Eve's experience exempli-
fies the sad fact that good and evil are bound up together:

> Good and evil we know in the field of this World grow up together
> almost inseparably; and the knowledge of good is so involv'd and
> interwoven with the knowledge of evill, and in so many cunning
> resemblances hardly to be discern'd, that those confused seeds which
> were impos'd on *Psyche* as an incessant labour to cull out, and sort
> asunder, were not more intermixt. It was out of the rinde of one
> apple tasted, that the knowledge of good and evill as two twins cleav-
> ing together leapt forth into the World. And perhaps that is the doom
> which *Adam* fell into of knowing good and evill, that is to say of know-
> ing good by evill. (*Riverside* 1006)

It is characteristic of Milton's prose to be so rich and metaphorical
that it can, like a poem, mix two archetypal but seemingly unrelated
figures like Adam from Judeo-Christian tradition and Psyche, Cu-
pid's spiritual mate in Greek mythology, just as Milton combined
the infant Jesus and the god Pan in the Nativity Ode. Milton can
also add his own myths to earlier archetypes in one and the same
sentence, with good and evil pictured as Siamese twins who, bonded
together, leap into the world. On top of that, Milton can create theological paradoxes in the midst of metaphors. The word "doom" makes

Adam's action out to be fatalistic, but the choice of knowing good by evil issues out of Adam's free will. There is so much going on in his prose sentences that they burst with baroque energy, like a Bach fugue carried by four vocal and various orchestral lines at the same time.

The great dining hall at Victoria College of the University of Toronto contains the full text of *Areopagitica*, as a ribbon or gold-leaf single-lined band running around the entire room. *Areopagitica* is one of the very few prose works ever written that might deserve to be printed as a single ribbon and followed around a large hall as one walks the text.

On January 30, 1649, King Charles I was executed by a decree of Parliament. So much for the divine right of kings. We do not know if Milton was present at the execution outside the Banqueting Room at Whitehall Palace. "It is at least possible," writes Milton's most recent biographer, Barbara Lewalski (224). The event assumed mythical proportions almost immediately. From the perspective of the Parliamentary government, the judicial execution of the king had to be demythologized. Charles could not be allowed to be a martyr.

The book supposedly written by the king as he lay in prison awaiting execution, *Eikon Basilike: The True Portraicture of His Sacred Majesty in his Solitudes and Sufferings* (actually by John Gauden as well-hidden ghost-writer), was put out as unashamed propaganda immediately after the king's death. By its title and its almost Roman Catholic image of Charles as a Christ figure gazing up at a heavenly crown, with attendant miracles, it made Charles seem godlike in his wisdom and self-sacrifice.

Milton answered the king's propaganda with *The Tenure of Kings and Magistrates*, written with blazing speed and published in mid-February 1649. Milton attempted to break or erase the icon of Charles the martyr by labeling him a tyrant and a wicked king – not at all a servant of his people as he should have been – who deserved to be deposed and put to death. The later tract with the famous name *Eikonoclastes* (1650) would do even more damage to the image of Charles I. Milton's purpose in both tracts was to stop the worship of the king by the "Image-doting rabble" (*Riverside* 1093).

The judicial execution of a king was such a momentous event throughout western Europe that Milton soon found himself the representative of a disreputable commonwealth government (a kind of military oligarchy, rather than a government built on a universal voting franchise). He had the uneasy task as representative of that commonwealth of justifying the execution of Charles I. An artist (in modern terms) with such a sensitive and well-tuned conscience must have felt occasional nausea at Cromwell's Interregnum government itself – a military dictatorship that occasionally massacred thousands of Irish citizens, broke the windows out of cathedrals, and forbade country dances or public dramatic performances. As a "brilliant and assiduous polemicist" (Corns, "Milton" 41), Milton used his own abilities as a writer and rhetorician to further the republican causes of righteous and god-fearing government responsible to the people.

Milton's voluntary work on *The Tenure* must have led to his appointment as chief polemicist for the Interregnum government, the person appointed by Parliament to write a *Defense of the English People* (1651) in Latin. As a defender of the unthinkable murder of a king, Milton became the personal target of anyone engaged in protecting European kings against damage to their reputation or personal harm. The political and moral arena was like that created by Shakespeare in *Richard II* and *Richard III* (a Shakespeare play that Milton seems to have especially liked): when should a weak king be deposed for the good of the people, and when should a tyrant king be defeated and killed by the will of the people? Though he was completely blind after 1651, Milton forced himself to continue the dirty business of defending his country and himself against the mud-slinging attacks of scholars hired by European governments to discredit England for what it had done to its king. Copies of his work were burned in places like Toulouse and Oxford (Campbell 220). His enemies declared that God had punished Milton for king-killing by blinding him, and he was reduced to being described as a blind dwarf. He had to fight back, personally, for the attacks on his government and on himself. He did so with sarcasm, with a nose for the smell of gossip about his enemies, and with the meanness of a junk-yard dog. He also found in his Latin prose the occasion to defend himself and to define his life's work, not only in his defense of the English people (1651) but in his defense of himself (1655). Milton's attacks on his enemies, the respected constitutional scholar Salmasius (Claude Saumaise) and the less respectable and lecherous cleric Alexander More, are vicious but funny, especially in their Latin puns – say on *morus* meaning "Moor" and "mulberry" at the same time, or

More's girlfriend's name Pontia, meaning "bridge," as something or someone who lies down for men. Though Milton received as much abuse as he gave, he retained his sense of humor in the international battle over whether or not a king might be deposed by the will of the people.

Plans for Tragedies: *Paradise Lost*

From the late 1630s on through the Restoration, in 1660, Milton had been planning to write tragedies based on events in English or Scottish history or on the Bible, and he may have had less certain plans for writing an epic, also based on events in the Old or New Testaments. The theme of temptation was certainly important, judging by his final choice of subjects: Adam and Eve tempted by Satan to disobey, Samson as husband and warrior tempted by pride and by his wife Dalila, and Jesus tempted by Satan in the wilderness, as described in Matthew 4:1–11. In what is now called the Trinity Manuscript, a collection of manuscript poems and notes for literary projects preserved in the library of Trinity College at Cambridge, Milton outlined biblical and historical subjects he considered using for tragedies that might serve to be instructional to his nation. He projected biblical tragedies focused on the Deluge, on John the Baptist, on Jephtha, on Solomon ruled by his wives, on Samson's marrying or Samson and the worshipers of Dagon, on Gideon as idol-breaker, on Tamar pregnant but condemned to death (Genesis 39:24), on the revolt of David against Saul or on David as adulterer with Bathsheba; and on the horrible fate of Ahab, his body eaten by dogs. With each of the more complete outlines for tragedies, Milton observes various Greek or Roman dramatic rules for presenting protagonists, antagonists, messengers, or choruses; he considers the unities of time, setting, and action; and he mentions plot devices such as epitasis (the development section in the middle of a play, as described by the Roman comedy writer Terence) or catastrophe.

Milton's titles of the various projected tragedies seem pretentious today, since they are often a mixture of proper names and obscure Greek terms, as in "Salomon Gynaecocratumenus" ("Solomon Governed by Women") or "Salomon Idolomargus" ("Solomon Crazy for Idols"). Milton would preserve one such tragic title in *Samson*

Agonistes, and we are lucky that *Paradise Lost* did not take Milton's earlier, awkward title "Adam Unparadized." Throughout his poetry- and prose-writing career, Milton made a habit of catching his reader's attention by exotic titles, as with *Colasterion* or *Tetrachordon* or *Samson Agonistes*.

In the outlines for tragedies, which editors date with some uncertainty in the early 1640s, Milton showed interest in political themes current in the 1640s – the power of church authorities, the susceptibility of kings to the influence of their wives, rebellion against tyranny – but he also showed a consistent interest in chaste or temperate living, in true religion as compared with idolatry, in liberty as opposed to licentiousness, and in patience as a heroic Christian virtue.

Why would Milton even have considered English or Scottish themes for tragedy? The obvious answer is that Shakespeare certainly did, but that answer would be glib, because Milton's interest in a tragedy on the subject of Macbeth or the history of King Lear (or Lir) is quite different from Shakespeare's, as if Milton never read either of Shakespeare's great tragedies, despite having written a memorial poem to Shakespeare for the Second Folio. Milton must have considered himself as a professional historian, since he was to write a *History of Britain* and a *History of Muscovia* (Russia). His tragedies would have been doctrinal or instructional to his country – more plays as conceived of by Puritan factions than by Shakespeare's anti-Puritan group of playwrights. *Samson Agonistes*, as the composer Handel was to understand when he set Milton's words to music, is as much of a sacred oratorio as it is a Greek tragedy. When we read Milton's retelling of the Macbeth story or the Lear story, we can see almost nothing of Shakespeare's plays in either account. In other words, when Milton conceives of tragedy, he does not seem to be thinking of Elizabethan tragedy at all. "L'Allegro" associates Shakespeare with comedy and Jonson with tragedy. By the 1640s Milton was thinking of tragedy in terms of instructive history or Bible stories that might also teach an English person valuable lessons about life. *Samson Agonistes* has more to do with Euripides and the Bible itself than it does with Shakespearean tragedy.

One major question for Milton critics concerns how three outlines for a tragedy on the fall of Adam and Eve became an epic, *Paradise Lost*. Milton had never lost sight of the importance of the story of the origin of evil; throughout his adult life he read in commentaries on Genesis that explained the Old Testament story in terms of its Christian interpretation, with the serpent being Satan, with Eve as counterpart to the Virgin Mary, and with Jesus Christ as the redeemer of humankind for the sin of Adam. In theological terms, Milton considered questions such as whether God's foreknowledge that Adam and Eve would sin had any effect on the destiny that allowed the sin. He had to provide motives for the serpent's temptation of Eve first and then Adam, and he had to provide dialogue between Eve and the Serpent, or rather Satan in the Serpent, now dignified by a capital letter in Christian dogma. He also had to provide motives for Adam and Eve to disobey the one commandment God instituted in Eden for Adam and Eve: "But of the tree of knowledge of good and evil, thou shalt not eat of it: for in the day that thou eatest thereof thou shalt surely die" (2:17). Milton and the commentators on Genesis had to work out exactly what a tree of knowledge of good and evil might look like or might mean as a symbol.

They needed to know exactly what it might mean to disobey God's one commandment. Milton does not name the tree "apple" for a calculated time, holding his reader in suspense in order to stress the disobedience more than to concentrate on the relatively trivial fruit. As for the tree, it is "Our death the tree of Knowledge" (4.221), a phrase which emphasizes the fact that knowledge is not always a good thing to have, especially when it is "Knowledge of good bought dear by knowing ill" (4.222).

Milton's theological niche

Milton is sometimes called an Arian, sometimes an Arminian, sometimes an Antitrinitarian, sometimes a Subordinationist, occasionally a Socinian, rarely a Unitarian, and almost never a Quaker. Each of those heretical schools has a history and a set of beliefs, many of which have to do with the three persons of the Holy Trinity – God the Father, God the Son, and God the Holy Ghost. To oversimplify things, Milton believed that the Father and Son both existed, but he was not sure about the precise nature of the Holy Ghost or Holy Spirit. He believed that God created the universe out of Himself, rather than out of nothing. He believed that the Son, incarnated as Jesus Christ, was created by the Father and clearly subordinated to the Father. The invocation to light at the beginning of Book 3 of *Paradise Lost* is rich and full of subtle theological distinctions, and it can be studied in detail by any student who would like to see Milton's theology at work in the epic. Whether Milton was a theologian first and a poet second, however, is another critical problem often shouted over but never resolved. Meanwhile, I have heard stories of Roman Catholic nuns praying to the spirit of Milton, despite all the horrid things he says about monks and nuns in his poetry and prose, and Milton seems to have an ecumenical appeal to Jews, Muslims, Hindus, Buddhists, and atheists alike.

Milton's theological school or brand of heresy is still hotly debated, and what is almost surely his manuscript book of private theology, entitled *De Doctrina Christiana*, not discovered until 1823, has a disputed provenance. There may even still exist a small school of critics who would like him to be an orthodox Anglican. (He was buried in the church where his father was buried, St. Giles, Cripplegate, in London, with his burial probably accompanied by the service for the dead spelled out in the Book of Common Prayer.) *De Doctrina Christiana*, a complicated mess of a manuscript, with many entries written in by many scribes, may itself be a compendium of theology first compiled by someone other than Milton but augmented by Milton by dictation to all those various scribes. A committee of scholars expert in everything from theology and seventeenth-century politics to computational linguistics is presently at work examining the manuscript of *De Doctrina Christiana*, to try to discover which parts of it are most likely to have been composed in Milton's careful Latin.

Milton's epic swirls from heaven to hell to earth, and it swirls backwards and forwards in time. The baroque is sometimes defined as art barely within control, or art at the boundaries of existence. The energy of *Paradise Lost* is incessantly moving (in both senses of the word), as in the famous oxymoron "darkness visible," with a restless energy. Milton's words are energetic through their puns (look at the word "fruit" in the second line), his phrases bear almost explosive weight, and his similes contain so much meaning that critics have discussed the Vallombrosa simile or the Norwegian pine simile ever since the first annotator of the epic wrote a commentary.

Milton's single words contain the richness of their etymology and their puns; his phrasing is the richest in the English language outside of Shakespeare's quotation-making aphorisms or great phrase-making in something as simple as "To be or not to be." And his images carry a baroque energy as surely as do the images of a Rubens or a Rembrandt. Probably the closest pictorial parallel to *Paradise Lost*, to go back one generation to Michelangelo, is in the end-panel of the Sistine Chapel, the image of Christ in Judgement, with hell and heaven spread out above his head and below his feet.

Paradise Lost begins in such turbulent baroque imagery, with the fallen angels "rowling in the fiery Gulfe / Confounded though immortal" (1. 52–3). The verb tenses bounce back and forth from the time of the Fall in "Brought" to the end of time in Christ's redemption with the verb "Restore" and then onward to the present time of the invocation, when the narrator can ask his muse to "Sing," all in four lines, with many other time zones included in the tenses – even before the first long sentence is completed.

Milton's blindness

Milton undoubtedly began outlining the tragedy that would become the epic *Paradise Lost* long before he became completely blind, in March of 1652, but by the mid-sixties he must have become used to the patient endurance that his condition enforced on him. The fact that the narrator is blind is imposed on the reader of Milton's epic from the very first, and Milton makes the best of it, comparing himself to the blind epic poet Homer or blind prophets such as Tiresias, given the gift of second sight to compensate for the loss of eyesight. Between Milton the blind prophet and seer and his muse, who brings divine inspiration, as with the spirit of God breathing creation into the water in the image of the dove brooding on her nest, the epic is made to seem prophetic and divinely inspired. Milton defines blindness spiritually, when the blind person, deprived of outer light, looks toward the inner light so sought after by various preachers or auto-biography writers identified as Puritans. He, or his inspiring Muse, sees "things invisible to mortal sight" (3.55).

But Milton also takes pains in *Paradise Lost* and also in *Samson Agonistes* to define blindness clinically. To a person who has his kind of blindness, a "drop serene" (3.25) he says, imposing the medical terminology of his time on his readers, causes light to be suffused. Milton's blindness could sense light but not shape. Modern medicine would define Milton's serene drop as glaucoma, which gradually blurs sight from the periphery of the eye to the center, like a spreading drop. The treatments for his blindness were barbaric, from the perspective of modern medicine. What was prescribed for the headaches that Milton suffered from periodically was seatoning, "piercing the skin just below the hairline, passing through the holes a hot cautery with a diamond point and then a needle with thread dipped in egg white and rose oil" (Lewalski 260).

Milton also defines being blind in terms of its psychological effects. Blindness causes a "damp" (compare *Paradise Lost* 9.45 with 11.544, with "damp" both as verb and noun) that, corresponding to the effect of bleak weather in England, sounds a great deal like the modern depression or affective seasonal disorder caused by lack of sunlight (or sight). Like many artists, especially poets, Milton may have been manic-depressive, working with enormous bursts of creative energy, though he was never delusional. The modern jargon term "obsessive-compulsive" might also characterize his attention to detail, and "anal-retentive" has also been used by psychological critics to describe his self-absorption and his retained memory of everything he had ever written. Critics still marvel at the fact that the blind Milton could remember what he had dictated in Book 2 of *Paradise Lost* even as he was dictating lines in Book 11.

A blind person senses the world differently from a sighted person, of course: sound becomes more important, as does the direction of sound. A blind person must practice echolocation, to detect the source of sounds. Voice becomes a key to the character of a speaker, and each character a blind man writes will have a distinctive and unique voice – as if that character has a voice print. Milton's characters do not sound like each other: when Adam and Eve begin to sound like Satan, they have lost part of their own character and assumed part of his. As with a wood at night, *Paradise Lost* is full of sounds that a human being suddenly placed in the dark must learn to interpret.

A blind musician may also write musical devices – tunes, airs, melodies, syncopated rhythms, and harmonies – into his words. If an acute reader learns to look for words used in their musical sense, words like *air* (4.264), *harmony* (7.560), *chorus* (7.275), *choir* (4.711), *note* (3.40), or *tune* (5.41), Milton will reward that reader with cues to his own word-music, with its diminuendos and crescendos, its staccato drumbeats of words, its deliberate meaningless monotony in the mouth of a monotonous character, its breathtaking musical beauty in the verbal equivalent of a hymn, a rhapsody, or a variation on a theme.

Good and bad smells are subtly important in the blind man's epic. Satan stinks, from time to time, as does death (10.272), and the flowers of Eden smell as good as they might appear to the sighted person (8.527). The taste of good or "savourie fruit" (5.304) is of course good, especially before the Fall, but Adam and Eve are also guilty of bad taste as well as disobedience when they taste the fruit of the Tree of Knowledge of Good and Evil.

Sight is treated almost nostalgically, by the blind narrator who has lost it:

> Thus with the Year
> Seasons return, but not to me returns
> Say, or the sweet approach of Ev'n or Morn,
> Or sight of vernal bloom, or Summers Rose
> Or flocks, or heards, or human face divine;
> But cloud in stead, and ever-during dark
> Surrounds me, from the chearful wayes of men
> Cut off, and for the Book of knowledg fair
> Presented with a Universal blank
> Of Natures works to mee expung'd and ras'd,
> And wisdome at one entrance quite shut out.
>
> (3.40–50)

Milton more than compensates for his blindness by amplifying all of the other senses, and remembering acutely the sighted world he had left in 1651. Milton had some comforts in his blindness: Edward Phillips describes "a pretty Garden-house in Petty-France in Westminster, next door to the Lord Scudamore's, and opening into St James Park," to which Milton moved on December 17, 1651 (plate 6).

As one can see in the passage on his blindness, and the sonnet on the same painful subject, Milton the man is hard to separate from his narrator. Far from being an impersonal "author-function," Milton is constantly in the face of the reader, imposing his own voice and his own will on readers. Reading or listening to *Paradise Lost* is an unnerving experience: a charismatic and frighteningly intelligent narrator is constantly telling you what to think, pushing you around,

Plate 6 Milton's house in Petty France, Westminster, in a nineteenth-century engraving published in the *Illustrated London News*, January 9, 1874.
© British Library, London.

allowing you to sin (if we believe Stanley Fish), but at the same time teaching you, increasing your knowledge, but without being a bully about it. The pushing and pulling can wrench a reader especially in the early books, when a reader must decide whether or not to admire Satan, the being who can say "to be weak is miserable / Doing or Suffering" (1.157–8), or take the narrator's word for it that Satan is "the Arch-fiend" and that he is saying what he is saying so that "with reiterated crimes he might / Heap on himself damnation" (209, 214–15). One other thing about Satan diminishes him and should not be forgotten: he is only God's errand boy. As he himself says, the fallen angels "do [God's] errands in the gloomy Deep" (1.152).

We are not sure what to call the narrator. At times he is certainly Milton, as when he complains that he is blind and surrounded by the threats that the poet was subject to after the Restoration of Charles II, but at other times his voice is close to that of his muse, divinely inspired and akin to the spirit who had also inspired Moses to write Genesis (according to seventeenth-century notions of biblical authorship). The narrator asks, in the invocation of Book 3, for "Celestial light / [to] Shine inward" (51–2), replacing his external blindness with internal light, but in the invocation to Book 7 he admits that he is "fall'n on evil days" and on "evil tongues," and that he is "in darkness, and with dangers compast round" (25–7). This is Milton the Regicide speaking, afraid for his life but confident of the divine inspiration issuing from his muse Urania. Yes, Milton the poet was in physical danger of being torn apart by a mob avenging the death of Charles I, and he had to overcome "an age too late, or cold / Climat, or Years" (9.44–5) – everything from the chilly and moist climate of England to his own advancing infirmity to an era that no longer appreciated epic poetry.

The narrator has also been called Milton's "organ voice," by which was meant a poetic voice possessing the range of tones of a pipe organ in a cathedral (the term was popular in the late nineteenth and early twentieth centuries), and his "epic voice" as he imitates Homer and Vergil, Dante, Tasso, and Ariosto. Milton's voice is, as he points out, a "mortal voice" (7.24) and not the biblical voice of God.

Milton may not permit us to become comfortable with any definitive name for his narrator: the pronoun "I" meaning "Milton" or narrator is only used at the beginning of Book 1, Book 3, Book 7, and Book 9. In every case, Milton is quick to discard the narrative

"I" for a dramatic "I," the voice of one of his characters. For instance, the "I" of Book 3 stops indicating the narrator by line 54; by
line 98 "I" is God the Father.

The relationship between Milton the human poet and his muse,
not named "Urania" until Book 9, is such a complex one that several books have been written about it. Psychoanalytic critics have
pointed out that Milton seems to shift genders in his autobiographical desire to be "milked" of his poetry, and he certainly wants to
subsume his own voice in that of his female muse. Yet he mentions
Urania only twice in *Paradise Lost*, as if embarrassed by the process of
naming her, and he insists that he is invoking "the meaning, not the
Name" (7.5), thereby denying the validity of the name Urania, usually given to the Muse of Christian poetry, by such poets as DuBartas.
Milton, unlike DuBartas, seems embarrassed by the association between his one true Christian muse and the widely distributed nine
pagan classical muses.

The epic virtues

Milton will not allow his readers to remain comfortable with the
traditional epic virtues of outward, glory-seeking, active anger and
aggressive boldness embodied in Achilles, Odysseus, and all their
Renaissance imitators. By contrast, Christ's sacrifice was passive,
lonely, quiet martyrdom, the model for all Christian behavior. In
Paradise Lost, Milton changes the direction of epic, rejecting what he
labeled the "tinsel trappings" of Renaissance romantic epic and the
militarism of the ancient epic. Even the gregariousness of the ancient epic hero will be cast aside for the solitude and isolation of
Adam and Eve, and then Jesus in *Paradise Regain'd*. In fact, any lonely,
morally isolated rebel against unjust authority may find Milton's
type of heroism – quiet, passive, noble, intensely private – very appealing.

The ideal of both epics is the "one just man" (11.890) – someone
like Noah, righteous and fearless, who resists the overwhelming evil
of the world. The representative of such virtue among the angels is
Abdiel, who adores God with such zeal that he can resist the evil of
all of Satan's legions, under tremendous social pressure, and remain
faithful to God even when he is utterly alone in his faith.

Milton's ideal of heroism is solitary, the act of the individual with faith and courage, someone who must stand against the majority opinion with great courage. That individual embodies what the narrator in *Paradise Lost* calls "the better fortitude / Of Patience and Heroic Martyrdom" (9.32). His better fortitude will usually be accompanied by the Christian virtues of "Temperance and Love" (12.583). In *Samson Agonistes*, Patience will be called "the truest fortitude" (654). All of Milton's dramatic heroes, from the Lady in the masque to Samson and the Jesus of *Paradise Regain'd*, will embody patience and, to some extent, heroic martyrdom. Lonely but righteous Old Testament prophets such as Jeremiah or Isaiah, John the Baptist, Jesus in the wilderness, the Lady alone in the woods, and Samson, all share the lonely heroism of the just. Over and over again in Milton's work, the words *patience, justice, hero, martyr, fortitude,* and *faith* are linked. Such lonely heroic isolation is hard for a sociable reader to accept at times.

The freedom of the individual to choose good or evil is essential for Milton's Christianity. The reasonable individual must make a moral choice. The choice for good or for evil defines our separation from or our link to God. In Milton's epic, Adam and Eve must choose to eat or not to eat the fruit of the tree of the knowledge of good and evil. They are tempted by Satan in the Serpent, but in the end they must each alone make the painful choice to disobey one simple, clear, easy to obey command – not to eat of that one fruit.

In stern terms, again hard for a modern reader to take or to understand, Milton's God in Book 3 makes it clear that Adam and Eve will sadly disobey the one easy commandment. In the process they will become ingrates, because they have been created free to choose and given a beautiful and idyllic place to live, the pleasurable Eden. Eve has been created for Adam at his request, as his helpmeet – his fitting and suitable companion, close to equal to him in her intellectual capacity though softer and more inclined to domesticity. There should be no problems between them, although God has also given them the potential to fall or the liability (in the legal sense) that they might fall: Eve may be inclined toward the vanity that will make her susceptible to the Serpent's flattery, and Adam might be inclined toward worshiping his wife's exterior beauty more than admiring her inner virtue. Such inherent human faults might incline them toward making mistakes, but when they choose to disobey God's one commandment, their sin includes every sin from greed and envy

to lust and murderousness. In one act, they murder the human race
at its genetic beginning, but that they do so is not God's fault. He
made them free to choose: otherwise they would have been pup-
pets. As Milton wrote in *Areopagitica*,

> many there be that complain of divin Providence for suffering *Adam*
> to transgresse, foolish tongues! when God gave him reason, he gave
> him freedom to choose, for reason is but choosing; he had bin else a
> meer artificiall *Adam*, such an *Adam* as he is in the motions [puppet
> shows]. (*Riverside* 1010)

Milton's God and Satan

Milton's God is a father, a creator, and a lover of humankind, his
children. As a world-maker, he is an artist, and all artists or creators
since have imitated him. It doesn't take a Freudian critic to see that
Milton wants his God to be a father figure, and someone not unlike
his own nurturing and supportive father. Milton's God is the patriarchal figure of authority. He may be pictured with the flowing white
beard of Michelangelo's God, creating Adam and Eve. But he is also
father and mother of Adam and Eve: he gives them both life, Adam
out of clay and Eve out of Adam. He guides the birth of Eve from
Adam's side, as if he were a benevolent and kind surgeon or obste-
trician, and he must be both father and mother to the first two humans he has created, nurturing them, providing a home, warning
them to avoid danger.

Of course, critics have seen that Milton's God sometimes speaks
in a shrill schoolmaster's voice, calling Adam and Eve "ingrate" and
fuming about the disobedience of his pupils. The relationship as
outlined by a prescient Father in Book 3 looks very much like an
authoritarian father faced by rebellious adolescent children. But
Milton's God is not a tyrant, and he is not quite the "patriarch" – at
least not in the negative sense of a natural-born exploitative, colonial warlord. Fathers, according to the homilies of the Anglican
Church, were supposed to have an innate authority over their wives
and their children in a natural hierarchy of excellence which was
rarely violated or reversed.

> This precept doth particulaire to the husband: for hee ought
> to be the leader and authour of loue, in cherishing and increasing

concord, which then shall take place, if hee will vse moderation and not tyranny, and if he yeelde some thing to the woman. For the woman is a weake creature, not indued with like strength and constancie of minde, therefore they be the sooner disquieted, and they be the more prone to all weake affections & dispositions of mind, more then men bee, & lighter they bee, and more vaine in their fantasies & opinions. These things must bee considered of the man, that hee be not too stiffe, so that he ought to winke at some thinges, and must gently expounde all things, and to forbeare. (*Certaine Sermons or Homilies appointed to be read in Churches, In the time of the late QueeneElizabeth of famous memory* [London, 1623])

According to the established church, in other words, the husband should be tolerant and forgiving toward his wife, because she is the weaker vessel, according to the Bible, and because she is more vain and lighter. To Milton's credit, from a twenty-first century perspective, he seems to paint Eve as not much weaker or more lightweight than Adam, even though she is defined in terms of her lower intellectual capacity and he is defined in terms of his masculine strength and authority. We are in a patriarchal system, no doubt, but it is not tyrannical, and it admits to the possibility of a conversation between husband and wife as first created and created helpmeet. Milton takes pains to define "helpmeet" as a fitting companion created just to complement male personality, with Eve being a kind of Yin to Adam's Yang.

"Satan he's a liar and a conjurer, too" – so run the words of an Appalachian folk song still sung in blue-grass circles. The characterization works well for Milton's Satan, however attractive he may seem at first to the reader. The appeal of Milton's Satan has always been based on his saying noble-sounding things like "Better to reign in Hell, then serve in Heav'n" (1.263), but when one thinks about the way he conjures with words like "reign," one can see that he is lying, that like the biblical Satan he is "a liar and the father of it" (John 8:44). One cannot really "reign" like a good king, not in Hell, which must sponsor tyranny more than any other form of government, if it is not just a chaos. Serving God in Heaven out of free will, on the other hand, is a joy, just as it is a joy for Adam and Eve to worship their creator in the Garden of Eden.

Satan's relationship with the other fallen angels (critics call them "fallen angels" instead of "devils" because Milton keeps reminding us of what they lost, their angelic stature, by their bad decision) is based on power games and betrayal, confidence games and lies. Satan is the great seducer (he leads people or other angels away from God), manipulator, and charismatic tyrant. Since the position of the tyrant is not one of inherent strength, he will be "the first in flight from pain" (4.921), a coward even when he seems to be brave in the process of "volunteering" to leave Hell in order to tempt Adam and Eve, whom Beelzebub calls the "punie habitants" (2.367) of earth. The volunteering is a sham or a confidence game, the act of courage is an act of cowardice, and the beings he is going to attack are puny, at least in physical strength, compared to a fallen angel. Satan even betrays his fellow fallen angels when he deserts the pain of Hell and leaves them all behind, wallowing in that fiery pit. He is a charlatan, a mountebank, a necromancer, and a fraud as he lies to all his associates, runs away from their pain, and attacks lesser beings in a much more pleasant world. His habit of lying is his strongest personal trait.

Like any tyrant, Satan has no true friend. His "mate" is Beelzebub, but even Beelzebub, despite being very much Satan's right-hand bad angel, will also be deserted as Satan flies from the pain of his own self-inflicted damnation. When Satan returns after seducing Adam and Eve, and again tries to use Beelzebub as his shill, he will be universally hissed even by the fallen angels, who have been transformed, by Milton's poetic justice, into hissing serpents.

The hell of Satan, though, is an internal hell, one that he carries with him wherever he goes. Whatever he runs from or wherever he runs to, he is his own hell. As he eloquently puts it, "Which way I flie is Hell: my self am Hell" (4.75). It isn't that Hell does not have a physical location. It does, though not in the center of Earth. But Satan also carries his own hell around with him, as do all beings with bad consciences.

The other fallen angels we meet as characters in Books 1 and 2 – Moloch, Mammon, and Belial – are all fragments of the personality of Satan, and they are all obsequious servants of the tyrant Satan. Moloch is the warlike component of Satan, who has himself led the forces in the revolt in Heaven. Mammon is the materialistic component of evil, the being who values things or possessions more than spirit, soul, or character. Belial is the sly, intellectual, and slothful fallen angel, someone who sounds good but is in himself an embodiment of the sins of Sloth, Envy, Covetousness, and Lust, all rolled into one useless being – a whining, complaining fallen angel, whose words promise more than he can deliver. In *Paradise Regain'd*, the various attributes of Belial, Moloch, and Mammon will be reunified in Satan as he tempts the Son of God, and he will be sly, sensuous, angry, and materialistic in turn.

Though Milton's Satan cannot be directly compared with the historical Charles II, he does fit the mold of the self-aggrandizing, posturing tyrant, very much in control of his own propaganda machine (Beelzebub is Goebbels to Satan's Hitler). He poses as a martyr just as he is hurting his own subjects and fellow creatures the most.

Satan can be proven to be a liar or a kind of confidence man, a conjurer, a cheat, a necromancer possessing the body of the Serpent, and then, in a way, possessing the body of Eve to tempt Adam with. His two principal motives are disreputable envy and revenge (what motives are more powerful in human experience?). Like most cowards, he aims his revenge not at his chief enemy, God, but at the weaker Adam and Eve, whom he envies because they have good and innocent desires and a beautiful relationship with one another – all satisfying and healthy states of well-being that he cannot have. Instead, all of his feelings are perverse, self-defeating, self-destructive, and pointless.

All sins are incorporated in Satan as the author of all evil. His authority or authorship is opposite to but not equal to the authority of God, or even the authority and authorship of Adam in relation to Eve (he is her author in the sense that she is created from him, to be subject to him). Being the author of evil, or the father of lies, is never as good being engaged in any positive activity.

The henchmen of Satan – Beelzebub, Mammon, Belial, Moloch – are just extensions of Satan's evil into other perverse territories, however much they represent universal human weaknesses or delusions. Worshipers of Baal or Mammon, Belial, and Moloch, as recorded in the Old Testament, are all deluded as compared to worshipers of what Milton would have considered the only true god. Each one of them represents a significant deviation from a good and purposeful life. To follow any one of them into materialism, sensuality, senseless violence, or idolatry would be a kind of madness, theologically speaking, but each of them represents a threatening state of mind, and together they add up to a moral chaos.

In addition to introducing types of evil in the fallen angels, Milton very cleverly transforms a biblical passage, "the wages of sin is death" (Romans 6:23), into disgusting physical allegory in which Satan gives birth to Sin, then Death rapes her incestuously, and makes war on his perverted father. James 1:15, adds to that "Then when lust hath conceived, it bringeth forth sin: and sin, when it is finished, bringeth forth death," giving a scriptural cue to Milton to link sin, lust, and death.

After the birth of Sin and Death, infernal hell-hounds incessantly crawl in and out of the womb of Sin, recapitulating the incestuous violation of Sin by Satan and by Death. Sin, in other words, is ugly, and it leads toward premature and horrible death. All is perverse between Satan and Sin, or between Sin and Death. We, the readers, are not in a plane of reality so simple as that of a medieval morality play: we are closer to the psychiatrist's couch, listening to the arrogant confessions of serial killers. The perversity of all the violated taboos – murder, incest, rape, and you-name-it deviations from healthy behavior – is as ugly human behavior as is imaginable.

Evil also spreads like a plague or infectious disease in *Paradise Lost*, and degenerative diseases are caused by evil living. The analogy works in any generation: degenerative diseases can be caused in part by overindulgence; degradation of the body causes physical, spiritual, or emotional problems; and plagues may be spread by immorality or promiscuity. Milton's image of the "Lazar-house" that begins at 11.749 seems depressingly familiar when any reader thinks of diseases humankind brings on itself.

The subplot of Satan's relationship with his daughter-spouse Sin and her son-lover Death is recapitulated in other odd places in *Paradise Lost*, and it might serve to illustrate Milton's echolocation of plots and themes in his epic, which begins in the middle of things and ends with a beginning (Adam and Eve leaving Eden to enter the world as the reader knows it). His plots often echo themselves without repeating themselves. The echoes may be present in one word that ties together various scenes and plots and themes. In the case of the scene that introduces Satan, Sin, and Death as a threesome, one word that echoes back and forth in the epic is "Author," which Sin uses to describe her unhealthy relationship with Satan, whom she labels as "my Father, [and] my Author" (2.864). Eve will describe Adam as "My Author and Disposer" (4.635), and God can be described as "Author of this universe" (8.360). The critical question is, what are we to make of the linking of good and evil through words like "Author?" Various plots and themes in the epic are linked by the word "Author," which does echo or reverberate as it points to the mirrored relationships between good authority and evil tyranny, between the creation of good and the creation of perverse evil.

> Good and evill we know in the field of this World grow up together almost inseparably; and the knowledge of good is so involv'd and interwoven with the knowledge of evill, and in so many cunning resemblances hardly to be discern'd, that those confused sees which were impos'd on *Psyche* as an incessant labour to cull out, and sort asunder, were not more intermixt. (*Riverside* 1006)

Through the use of the motif embodied in the word "Author," we are given echoes of events of creation or generation that are good and those that are evil, and we are encouraged to see good and evil growing in the field of the world intertwined and inseparable.

The plot and time scheme of *Paradise Lost* are so much of an interwoven tapestry or web from the mind of its author as to be very difficult to deconstruct or unweave. Milton seems to run his reader very close to the abyss of chaos, only to preserve an order or a storyboard that he seems to have firmly under control – especially with respect to the amount of time Adam and Eve spend in Paradise (Zivley). There are now 12 books in *Paradise Lost* (since the 1674 edition gave them to us), but there were 10 to begin with. Is the change from 10 to 12 significant numerologically? How could it be, if all significance in numbers, as with the center of the poem, were lost between the 1667 and 1674 editions? And what is the significance of Milton's including invocations, or something like invocations, at the beginning of Books 1, 3, 7, and 9? How was the positioning of those invocations altered when 10 books were changed to 12? Could a blind poet have worked out the structure of 12 new books of the epic with anything like geometrical precision? Or does Milton's organization proceed the way his mind worked – by musical echoes, vibrations, and reverberations? The images that have most impressed me for critical understanding of Milton's epic, as you can see, are motif, theme, echo, and reverberation, from music, and visual images from a cyclical series of narrative paintings such as that depicted in Michelangelo's Sistine Chapel frescoes, and tapestry (as in an oriental rug, at once traditional and individual, or a Jacquard pattern from a loom, conceived by humans but almost like a computer-generated image in its precise repetition).

Perhaps combativeness or feistiness would be better terms for Milton's competitive nature. He would not pick a fight, say, about religion, but if a Jesuit priest in Rome were to denigrate English Protestantism, Milton would engage that priest in fierce and aggressive verbal combat. Milton's stance was often that of the combative David against some huge and ungainly, or more likely ignorant or less learned, Goliath. Milton assumed the mantle of David when he defended the English people, then himself, against the attacks of the formidable French scholar Claude Saumaise, or Salmasius, and his sidekick Alexander More, called "Morus" in Latin. According to Salmasius, the blood of murdered kings would cry out against the injustice of violating a sacred bond between king and people. According to Milton, defending England's Parliamentary government against European monarchists, a king was nothing more than a high elected official who had to earn the trust and the respect of his people, and a tyrant is contemptible enough, because of the violation of that trust, that he may be executed legally, by the will of the people.

Milton takes battles like this large one over monarchy very personally. What was at first an attack on England and on its rule by Parliament, Protector, and army, becomes an attack on Milton himself, who stands for the country and fights for it as an individual. The malicious and combative Milton, attacked by various political opponents as having been struck blind for his arrogant wrongheadedness, goes after Salmasius and More on a gut level, accusing Salmasius of being less than a man in his relationship with his wife and accusing More of incessant promiscuity with maidservants (of which he was probably quite guilty). What began as a scholarly argument over the rights of people to depose their kings ends up as a very funny personal squabble between academic infighters.

It is hard to defend Milton's infighting or waspishness in taking all of his battles for liberty so personally, but his combativeness is a trait that makes him seem ever so human to a modern reader. His reduction of important theological matters, such as the imagined sting of death, to the personal level does humanize his poetry, as with the fear of unmemorialized death that the narrator of "Lycidas" expresses with his authorial "I." And the blindness of the narrator of *Paradise*

Lost is sometimes an intensely personal business, when one considers that Milton after the Restoration was isolated, threatened in Parliament and in danger at home, blind, and helpless – except for the power of his intellect and the courage of an old rebel. Milton has the talent to turn personal misfortune into universal, tragic human experience. He is not just a blind prophet and epic poet like Tiresias or Homer, he is a defenseless English poet, fallen on hard times in dark days.

Milton self-consciously wrote his own public-relations reports or propaganda throughout his life. He donated copies of his books to the Bodleian Library in Oxford, knowing that they would likely be preserved there; he preserved his own juvenile poetry, so that biographers would be able to discuss his early signs of genius; he trained his nephews to preserve his memory, and he took care that his pupils and amanuenses knew what he was reading and writing; in public life, he left a paper trail in which even his spelling practices were outspokenly preserved. He met and knew his printers; no other poet of his century, with the exception of Ben Jonson, knew so much about how books were constructed, contracted for, or sold, much less ornamented or configured with explanatory apparatus. Milton's friendship with George Thomason, though probably not calculated, may have had something to do with the fact that Thomason was an archivist, collecting all the ephemeral political pamphlets published in the 1640s and 1650s. (The "Thomason Tracts" are now preserved in the British Library.) Milton's 1645 *Poems* volume was so carefully constructed that it included the original and the translation of a Latin ode by Horace on facing pages, and his *Areopagitica*, itself about the politics of printing, was printed with carefully controlled marginalia that do seem to be under control of the author as well as the printer.

When Milton wrote propaganda for the Interregnum government under his own name, that propaganda was always personalized and proudly signed, with markings of the individual poet, scholar, political theorist, theologian on every page. Milton wanted to be preserved as a courageous man, an independent thinker, a nonconformist (beyond the religious sense of that term) – in short, as an original. We would have to conclude that his ego (as compared with that of Shakespeare) was remarkably strong and evident in everything he wrote.

Though a Jacobean schoolboy might have been expected to

memorize more of his lessons, perhaps chanting declensions or con-
jugations as a group in rhythmical patterns, than does a modern school
child, Milton seems to have retained a remarkable amount of what
he read. Like the Greek philosophers, he allowed Memory to be a
goddess, at worst "Dame Memory and her *Siren* daughters" (*Yale*
1.820) and at best Mnemosyne, said in Greek mythology to be the
mother (by Zeus) of the Seven Muses. She is referred to in Milton's
Latin poem "De Idea Platonica," as "Memory, most blessed mother
of the nine goddesses" (*Riverside* 221). It may be too easy to say that
Milton worshiped memory, but he did possess a phenomenal memory.
He seems to have memorized his own Latin poems, so that he could
recite some of them at the Italian academies he was invited to
address in 1638, and he retained everything he read in memory,
even after he went blind, so that he was able to dictate entries in his
own commonplace book from books he had in memory, with a precision that allows a modern scholar to identify a text according to
how Milton quoted it. His prose is crammed with allusions to what
he remembers having read, and he is perhaps the most thoroughly
allusive poet who ever wrote to be understood in English.

Slow reading, on purpose

It has become fashionable in recent years to hold marathon readings of *Paradise Lost*, from Otago to Chicago. The process takes about
ten hours, but those who stick to the end and listen to the entire
poem read aloud report a new level of understanding about the poem.
Even with imperfect readers or readers whose native tongue is not
English, it is good to read the poem word by word, and to listen or
form the sounds of every word. Readers can come to understand
how the poem is intended for the ear rather than just the mind's
eye, and they realize how dramatic the poem is. It is a series of
speeches, from many points of view, good and evil, with advice from
the narrator as a reliable chorus. Above all, it is to be heard and
concentrated on, as with the best of Shakespeare's soliloquys. It demands complete attention, and the best way to read it with understanding is to read it aloud.

As Milton described an effective poetic style, his epic is "simple,
sensuous, and passionate" (*Of Education*; *Riverside* 984). Each of those
adjectives describes a style that could easily be twisted to evil pur-

poses, and Milton is aware of that. Simplicity might indicate simple-mindedness or gullibility; sensuousness might divert a reader from the spiritual; and passion, of course, could be highly suspect, as when Adam is overly passionate about Eve. Each of the elements of successful poetic style needs to be balance. It won't do to have God speak too sensuously: that job might be Satan's at his most tempting, when he is breathing in Eve's ear. And if God speaks simply, godly simplicity must be plain, clear, unequivocal, dignified, and authoritative.

The style of *Paradise Lost* changes significantly when Satan, or someone who works for Satan or has been influenced by him, is speaking. The style becomes sensuously deceptive. "I should be much for open Warr, O Peers, / As not behind in hate" (2.119–20), says the fallen angel Belial, and we can already hear a sneer in his smooth voice; the narrator will later comment "Thus *Belial* with words cloath'd in reasons garb / Counsel'd ignoble ease, and peaceful sloath, / Not peace" (226–8). Belial's style is demonic in that it emulates reasonable speech and even appears to be good oratory, but it is really only a lame defense of ease and sloth. There is an identifiable demonic style in the epic: it uses degraded language, it is misleading on purpose, and it always leads the reader in a bad direction.

Perhaps the main problem with the speaking style of the principal speaking characters in *Paradise Lost* is with tone. How should God speak, for instance? God describes how Satan will corrupt humankind when we first hear him speak in Book 3. Satan will attempt to discover

> If him by force he can destroy, or worse,
> By some false guile pervert; and shall pervert
> For man will hark'n to his glozing lyes,
> And easily transgress the sole Command,
> Sole pledge of his obedience: So will fall,
> Hee and his faithless Progenie: whose fault?
> Whose but his own? Ingrate, he had of mee
> All he could have; I made him just and right,
> Sufficient to have stood, though free to fall.
>
> (ll. 93–9)

Critics sympathetic with Milton's theology and dramaturgy still worry about the way his God speaks from the beginning. We know how we should interpret God's first speech, but phrases like "false guile" and "glozing lyes" and "faithless Progenie," and nouns like "Ingrate" or verbs like "pervert" are bothersome.

What God says in predicting the ingratitude of Adam and Eve is very close in tone and content to what the narrator says when analyzing the motivation of Satan. The narrative voice is close to the voice of God, speaking about such things as Satan's methods and procedures. Just as it is a fact that Adam and Eve are ingrates, it is a fact that Satan will proceed either by force or guile, and that he will choose to pervert man by using lies that look like biblical glosses. But Alexander Pope was correct to infer that Milton's God sounds like a schoolmaster at times. Mischievously, biographical critics can remember that Milton himself was a schoolmaster and say that Milton's God merely sounds like Milton when he was being most schoolmasterish or pedantic. Again, the reasonable critic has to admit that what Milton's God says here is the truth – that humankind will listen to Satan's lies, despite having been fully warned that there is a danger from an evil master of disguises, and it is true that humans will become ingrates by disobeying the one simple command in Paradise, that they should not eat the fruit from one tree. Still, there is something harsh in God's words, "Ingrate, he had of mee / All he could have," as if God sounds like the mother or the father of a teenaged rebel.

Readers since Pope, readers in every generation of those who admire Milton but have problems with his God, may find God's tone annoying, even though what he says is the theological truth and the epic truth. Readers who are especially annoyed with Milton's God might read the brilliant *Milton's God* by William Empson, for ammunition in the war against God, and readers who would *like* to like Milton's God should read Dennis Danielson's *Milton's Good God* for a full justification of God's actions and tone in *Paradise Lost.* It is tempting to say that Milton's God is what the Christian God is supposed to be – omniscient, omnipotent, and omnipresent – and leave it at that; but Milton's God may require years of reading the epic to come to terms with.

Epic similes

In Milton's hands, the epic simile familiar from Homer or from Vergil is amplified, given reverberations and echoes. The link between tenor and vehicle, against the thing being compared and the thing it is being compared to, can be so extensive and exhaustive that Milton will use every conceivable connection between leaves randomly falling in a brook in Vallombrosa and fallen angels, entranced, rolling in a fiery lake in Hell. The varieties of evil become as numberless as leaves in autumn, and even the name Vallombrosa, suggesting the biblical valley of the shadow of death, is used as part of the economy of the comparison between leaves and fallen angels. The leaves are dead before they hit the water. The water carries them at random. The fall of the leaves seems to be careless, as they strew the brooks, but there is a godly design behind their distribution, no matter how chaotic it may look. The more the reader thinks about such extended similes, the richer they become.

Milton is well aware that Homer used a leaf simile (*Iliad* 6.146–9) to compare the numberless generations of human beings to leaves on the trees and leaves on the ground and that Vergil used an autumnal leaf simile to describe a huge crowd of people (6.305–10). He is also well aware that dry, yellow leaves or fallen leaves signify death, as when Macbeth talks about his own deadly way of life falling into the "sere, the yellow leaf." Milton's simile, a vital and original image, nevertheless includes all previous images of the same sort within itself. Within that one image, Milton competes with and replaces all earlier imagery on the subject, replacing pagan with Christian and overlaying lesser artistry with more far-reaching artistry. He writes the simile to end all similes.

Milton's poetry lends itself to close and precise reading of the text, within its own created context (the rest of the poem) and within the context of all the poetry it echoes and improves on. From the earliest close-reading editors, Patrick Hume, the Richardsons, and Bishop Thomas Newton, and critics and writers such as John Dryden, Joseph Addison, and Alexander Pope, *Paradise Lost* has been closely and meticulously examined, as Milton seems to have planned it to be, since he provided his own summary in the Arguments he wrote for each book. Each line of the poem, each phrase, each word carefully fit into place has been meticulously prearranged by a blind poet with prodigious powers of memory. The poet seems to hold the entire poem in his head. Milton seems to have had the ability to remember every line he had written, as if he were writing in stone from his earliest poetry, as he remembered and recited his Latin verses to the academies in Italy when he was asked to recite his own work there.

The reader of Milton's epics is forced to read closely, then, and to remember every earlier word or phrase that the poet has written, since each time Milton repeats a word or phrase or image he has used before the repetition will be incremental: it will add a new level of meaning. Milton's poetry demands complete concentration, as if he were forcing his fit reader to remember as much as a blind man remembers. Milton preserves so much of his own poetry in manuscript or in images practiced in prose before they were converted back into poetry that we readers cannot let our attention lapse for a second: the more the reader emulates the memory of Milton, the more meaning the poetry releases.

Also, the more the reader of Milton reads in the Bible, in the Homeric epics, in *The Aeneid*, in *The Faerie Queene*, the more allusive force the words of *Paradise Lost* will convey. Forever playing with words, a deep linguist and lexicographer, Milton never stops teasing his reader in prose or poetry with the entire etymological history of any important word he is using. He is a serious punster, and I would not put it past him to think of Adam's being deceived in terms of Adam's being "dis-Eved." Etymological critics have found puns in the "Dis" in "disobedience," indicating plausibly that Hell, "Dis," may be buried in the act of disobedience, and some have even found a pun bordering on the ridiculous in "disoBEDience." Eve is certainly "deflowered," in that her garden is taken away when she is cast out of Eden: the problem is to determine in what sense might she have been deflowered legally or sexually. Did Satan in some ways destroy her innocence, or rape her mind?

There are probably demonstrable puns in *Paradise Lost* based on Hebrew etymology (there may be very serious puns based on the various names of God), on Greek-derived words such as "spirit," on theologically rich words such as "grace" or "mercy" (think of what "merci" might convey in French). Milton establishes meanings in English words based on what the roots of the words might mean in Greek, Latin, Italian, French, or Spanish. Translators of Milton's poetry into Spanish or Italian – since he favored Romance languages – have always found their own language echoed in Milton's English etymologies.

Part of what gives Milton's poetry its baroque energy, its elusive

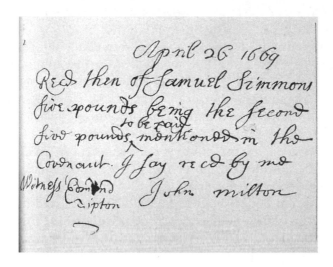

Plate 7 Samuel Simmons's receipt for payment to Milton for *Paradise Lost*.
From S. L. Sotheby, *Ramblings in the Elucidation of the Autograph of Milton*
(London: Thomas Richards, 1861). © British Library, London.

force, and great depth is in its word-choice. Words always have more
than their surface meaning in Milton's poetry. If one reads the entire King James Bible just in preparation for reading *Paradise Lost*,
the exercise is rewarding in that the epic will seem to be a series of
echoes of the meanings of words in a book that Milton knew by
heart. The same phenomenon occurs if one reads *The Iliad* or Ovid's
Metamorphoses. For that matter, one might prepare for reading Milton
by reading the entries for a number of key words in *Paradise Lost* in
the *Oxford English Dictionary*. James Joyce was supposed to have enjoyed reading in the *Oxford English Dictionary*: Milton could be said to
have written it (he is the third most-cited author, after Shakespeare
and Sir Walter Scott, in the *OED*).

Milton famously received £5 increments for his effort in writing
Paradise Lost (plate 7). The contract seems to make a case for great
literature's being undervalued, then as now, and it is true that
Milton's printers in the late seventeenth century and in the eighteenth century did make large sums of money on the printing of the
epic and his other works, without having to send royalties to Milton's
heirs. But Milton was undoubtedly hard-pressed for money after the
Restoration of Charles II in 1660, and he was a dangerous author to

print, his works subject to censorship and harassment because he had been labeled a regicide. Biographers and historians of the book have written that he was lucky to have received £10 for his efforts. In an age when laws protecting copyright were just coming into use, Milton was at least given a contract and he and his surviving wife were paid something for his work. There is some evidence that Milton was trying to make some money from his writing toward the end of his life, perhaps to protect his wife and children with a small estate, though his publishing career never seems to have been designed to support him, and he is in no danger at all of ever being labeled a hack writer or a writer for profit.

Several recent books about Milton have investigated the themes of imperialism, which in this case can be defined as the furthering of what would come to be known as the British Empire, and colonialism, in the sense of the responsibility for English colonies as in Ireland, Bermuda, or New England, in Milton's works. Martin Evans compares Milton's epics with Spanish and Portuguese epics of colonial conquest in order to determine how Milton may have perceived the natives of North America as compared with innocent Adam and Eve, and Balachandra Rajan and Elizabeth Sauer collected essays on the subjects of British colonialism in India or the Americas. Milton was well-acquainted with the ideal of island colonies or New World outposts as places of religious refuge. After all, Milton knew William Penn, soon to be of Pennsylvania, and he was tutored in the Dutch language in exchange for tutoring Roger Williams in several other languages (Campbell 155), between Williams's many trips to the New World. Both Milton and Andrew Marvell were well aware of the possibility of deportation from England to the colonies, as punishment for religious or political opinions, and Marvell's wonderful poem "Bermudas" expresses some of the ambiguities of Puritan flight from the rage of prelates "Unto an Isle so long unknown, / And yet far kinder than our own" (Marvell 18). Milton speaks of America in almost exactly the same terms, as a place whose very deserts might "hide and shelter" refugees "from the fury of the Bishops" (*Of Reformation*; *Yale* 1.585). It is no accident that Columbus is one of the very few near-contemporaries mentioned in *Paradise Lost*, and it is no accident that Milton consorted with Quakers such as Thomas Ellwood and William Penn after the Restoration of Charles II.

Whether Milton was a bloodthirsty colonial himself is still open to debate, because he can be quite brutal when discussing the Roman Catholic Irish, or when discussing military retribution for the colonial sins of Roman Catholic conquest, as when papal troops committed atrocities against the Waldensian sects in Piedmont, occasioning Milton's famous call to arms, "Avenge O Lord thy slaughter'd Saints" (*Riverside* 255). And Milton could use the word "savages" as well as any of his contemporaries, in a phrase like "mixt Rabble, part Papists, part Fugitives, and part Savages" to describe an Irish mob fighting against British rule (*Articles of Peace*; *Yale* 3.315).

Milton was not, however, a cruel or inhumane taskmaster himself, as a father, as a schoolmaster (he did whip his pupils, as did most schoolmasters of his time), or in his appointed roles as polemicist, poet, or theologian; and he applauded civilization insofar as it supported high art, lawfulness, gentility, and kindness (as compared with barbarous dissonance and violent mob rule). We would not expect such a person to endorse colonial cruelty, exploitation, and rape of people or environment. A case has even been made for Milton as radical environmentalist far in advance of the popular modern green movement, in the sense that he defended the innocence and inviolability of the natural world as he pictured it before the Fall in *Paradise Lost*. Since Milton is acutely aware of the natural world, to the point where he is acknowledged to be ahead of his time in his scientific curiosity about the nature and habits of plants, insects, and animals, we might be forgiven for calling him a proto-environmentalist.

It is difficult to decide for once and for all whether Milton supported the institution of monarchy, especially because it was the system he lived with throughout his life, even under the Protectorate of Oliver Cromwell, who was offered the crown (and famously declined to wear it). Milton's argument over kingship was not with whether it should exist but with whether the king should serve the people. Though the king was not elected, Milton saw the monarchy as existing for the benefit of the people, and the king as accountable to the people. The king should be a public servant in the best sense of the term. The supposed divine right of kings represented popular superstition, the "frivolous pretences of divine right" as in the collection of tithes by the church in conjunction with a monarch (*Considerations Touching the Likeliest Means to Remove Hirelings out of the Church*; *Yale* 7.296). To say that kings are accountable only to God, "is the overturning of all Law and government," and an unaccountable monarchy, he believed, "is the worst sort of tyranny" (*Tenure of Kings and Magistrates; Yale* 3.204). Kingship might be inevitable, given the available political systems of the late seventeenth century, but kings should rule by the consent of the governed.

"Paradise Found" (*Paradise Regain'd*)

According to Milton's young tutorial student and amanuensis, the Quaker Thomas Ellwood, it was a question put to Milton that provoked or inspired him to write the four-book epic on the subject of Paradise found. After Ellwood had been given the manuscript of *Paradise Lost* to take home to read, at Chalfont St. Giles, in August of 1665, and after he had "with the best intention, read it through," he went back to Milton and was asked how he liked the poem; then Ellwood "modestly but freely told him: and after some further Discourse about it, I pleasantly said to him, Thou hast said much here of *Paradise lost*, but what hast thou to say of *Paradise found?*" Milton "made [him] no Answer but sate sometime in a Muse; then brake off that Discourse, and fell upon another Subject" (Ellwood 199).

When Ellwood, perhaps a year later, visited Milton in London, Milton "shewed me his Second Poem, called PARADISE REGAINED, and in a pleasant Tone said to me, *This is owing to you: for you put it into my Head, by the Question you put to me at* Chalfont; *which before I had not thought of*" (Ellwood 200). If the manuscript of *Paradise Regain'd* was indeed complete by 1666, it was composed with amazing speed.

Biographers and literary critics ever since Ellwood's autobiography was first known have wondered how seriously to take his story. Since Ellwood seems a naive pupil if not exactly a simpleton, there is no reason to think he is promoting himself by making himself a sponsor or promoter of Milton's sequel to *Paradise Lost*. Ellwood was something of a poet himself, and he wrote the first elegy in memory of Milton (in very bad doggerel). Biographers often still assume that Milton was having a joke on Ellwood or flattering him, first by showing him his masterpiece, then by telling the young man that his question inspired the short epic. But there is no reason to suspect Ellwood's integrity, and he may well have put it into Milton's mind that a paradise lost needs to be followed by a paradise found.

Milton's plot is extrapolated from a biblical passage that takes up only about a third of chapter 4 in the Gospel of Luke:

And Jesus being full of the Holy Ghost returned from Jordan, and was led by the Spirit into the wilderness.

Being forty days tempted of the devil. And in those days he did eat nothing: and when they were ended, he afterward hungered.

And the devil said unto him, If thou be the Son of God, command this stone that it be made bread.

And Jesus answered him, saying, It is written, That man shall not live by bread alone, but by every word of God.

And the devil, taking him up into an high mountain, shewed unto him all the kingdoms of the world in a moment of time.

And the devil said unto him, All this power will I give thee, and the glory of them: for that is delivered unto me; and to whomsoever I sill, I give it.

If thou therefore wilt worship me, all shall be thine.

And Jesus answered and said unto him, Get thee behind me, Satan: for it is written,

Thou shalt worship the Lord thy God, and him only shalt thou serve.

And he brought him to Jerusalem, and set him on a pinnacle of the temple, and said unto him, if thou be the Son of God, cast thyself down from hence:

For it is written, He shall give his angels charge over thee, to keep thee:

And in their hands they shall bear thee up, lest at any time thou dash thy foot against a stone.

And Jesus answering said unto him, It is said, Thou shalt not tempt the Lord thy God.

And when the devil had ended all the temptation, he departed from him for a season.

It is obvious here that Milton adds to but does not subtract from the biblical narrative (which is, of course, repeated in the other Gospels). Very significantly, he adds the Temptation of Athens to the group. And he gives his short epic dramatic structure by having Satan discuss his strategy beforehand with Belial and by adding the conversation between the Son and his mother Mary. Each scene of temptation is a small struggle or agon, presented as if in a play, with the narrator serving as prologue, chorus, and commentator. The outcome is more of a comedy in the sense of *Divine Comedy*, in that good wins in the end.

The governing structure or frame is that of the brief epic, an answer to the diffuse epic, *Paradise Lost*. It is the story of obedience and success, whereas *Paradise Lost* was the story of disobedience and failure. It is the story of the Son's triumph over Satan, the fulfillment of the prophecy that the Seed of Eve and Mary will crush the Serpent of Genesis under his heel.

In a sense, Milton gives two for the price of one, once again, by combining genres and by housing *Paradise Regain'd* and *Samson Agonistes* under the one small roof of the 1671 volume. The two works go well together, and they are thematically connected, both being the struggle of one just man or one righteous individual against various temptations to do evil. As a dramatic poem, *Samson Agonistes* has more dramatic tension built into it, and Milton can interpret the Old Testament story with more freedom and complexity than he can interpret a Gospel story directly concerning Jesus. Milton's dramatic poem also has a tremendous catastrophe to bring it to a crashing climax. But the quieter story of the one-on-one temptation of the Son in the desert has value as an intimate and dignified struggle, and Milton takes pains to make his Son of God into a recognizable human who can demonstrate anger, scorn, and sardonic humor towards Satan on the one hand, or tender love toward his mother.

Of course, there is an autobiographical element in the brief epic. Frankly, the more one knows about Milton's life and prose writing, the more the Son sounds like John Milton – as precocious young man, as arrogant student, as bold adult controversialist never afraid to speak his mind, as wise old man who must reject the pagan idols of his youth. The Son even sounds at times like John Milton at the Restoration, disillusioned with the voice of ignorant people clamoring for freedom but not understanding what freedom means.

The main problem with Milton's brief epic is with the character of his Jesus, who is cold and rational as he repulses the temptations of Satan. Milton's Jesus, in resisting evil in the desert, is the one obedient man matched against the one disobedient man in Eden, Adam. Milton's Jesus is austere, tough-minded, rough on evil, and without sympathy for Satan, even in disguise.

As in Milton's masque, evil first appears in the disguise of a harmless peasant, but the Son of God sees through the disguise quickly and easily. Milton's Jesus or Son of God is not given the more honorific title of Christ, on purpose, in *Paradise Regain'd*. He is Jesus, the beloved Son of God instead, and he is Mary's son, sometimes the biblical Son of David, often Saviour, less often Messiah. Only once is he given all his titles, "Jesus Messiah Son of God" (2.4) in one lump.

Milton follows conventional typology in matching Adam and Eve in Eden with the Son in the "wast Wilderness" of the desert. The narrator immediately announces the apparent irony that Eden is raised again in the desert where the Son is tempted. The narrator also exults in the fact that the Son's heroic deed is accomplished secretly, privately, in isolation. Spiritual warfare, above the heroism of earlier epics, occurs so quietly that it has, at least according to Milton, been left "unrecorded" (1.16), at least by epic poets. The illusion cultivated by the narrator – Milton's boast – is that he will be the first epic poet or poet of stature to record the spiritual war between the Son and Satan, as he claimed to be the first to sing of "things unattempted yet," especially patience and heroic martyrdom, in *Paradise Lost*.

The main struggle in the brief epic is a skillful debate between worthy opponents, in the best British academic tradition. Though Satan and the Son are talking in private and in the desert, they debate with the style of parliamentarians, declaiming their long and eloquent speeches without embarrassment.

The shorter, demonic debate that precedes the main match in *Paradise Regain'd*, the one between Satan and his most oleaginous general, Belial, amuses a savvy reader. Watching the fallen angels discussing lust as a temptation for a perfect man is like watching trapped frogs in a barrel. Belial, being the fleshy devil he was in *Paradise Lost*, is obsessed with tempting the Son with lusts of the flesh, and he pictures degenerate women to be used for that purpose. His advice to Satan is to "Set women in his eye," which seems absurd when the reader knows that the Son is a perfect man, not susceptible to temptations on a human scale. It is curious that Satan rejects Belial's advice quickly, but then himself plagiarizes Belial's idea and conjures up the illusion of beautiful young women and men as part of a food temptation to satisfy the real hunger caused by the Son's fasting in the desert. That will not work either.

In the short epic, Mammon and Moloch are dispensed with, and Belial takes the place of Beelzebub as Satan's right-hand fallen angel, suggesting many types of demonic temptations rolled into a few sins of the flesh. Comus had tried the same sorts of tricks as Belial suggests and later Satan attempts, in the masque, and Comus also works with juggler's illusions. Satan had also exercised the same neon sensuality when he did tricks for Eve in the gilded disguise of the Serpent while tempting her to eat the fruit. But, according to a misogynistic Satan, that effort was designed to overcome Adam's "facile consort" Eve. What fooled Eve or Adam (Eve's beauty did that) just will not work on the Son of God.

The Son of God is a perfect man, literally holier than thou, or holier than anyone on earth. Even though he is subordinate to his Father and takes orders from him without understanding everything about his mission on earth, the Son is a perfect son, and, like Milton's Samson, he knows he is born to serve some great purpose.

We know from *Paradise Lost* and from Milton's theological treatise *On Christian Doctrine* that Milton's Son is subordinated to the Father, that he is thoroughly human in his incarnation, and that he is capable of real anger and real human love for his family. Once again, Milton bravely tackles the problem of anthropomorphism – how to present a god or a god-man who speaks a human language and takes on humanity in his incarnation. God calls his son "This perfect Man, by merit call'd my Son" (1.166). In other words, not only is the Son the son of God, he is perfect in his own right and he deserves to be called the Son of God.

Milton's Son of God – the dramatic character – cannot have too much of a human sense of humor, though he is allowed to speak the famous funny rebuff to Satan, "Mee worse then wet thou findst not" (4.486), after being transported through the air by another magic trick, and his answer certainly sounds like human sarcasm. Most of the time when he responds to Satan's various temptations, the Son sounds like anyone resisting temptation virtuously:

- how dare you show me these things;
- it is easy for someone like me to say no; or
- you needn't have bothered.

If he sounds self-righteous, that is because he was born righteous and because Satan's temptations are outrageous, like telling someone who has taken a vow of chastity, poverty, and obedience to eat, drink, be merry, and to forget the authority of God. The Son is not an abstinent monk or nun, but he has no need for the usual weaknesses of the flesh such as overeating, acquiring ostentatious jewelry, or gaping at handsome-looking men or women.

As twentieth-century librettists and script-writers have discovered, it is still difficult to present the character of Jesus Christ on stage, in the movies, or in any speaking part, whether or not Jesus is a Superstar. There is a real danger in modern cinema that a Jesus character will look or sound like a useless or pretentious fellow, a twit, a nerd, a drugged-out hippie, or, perhaps worst of all, a self-righteous Jesus-freak. To his credit, Milton did not succumb to the temptation to make his Son of God sanctimonious, preacherly, puritanical, hypocritical, pompous, or pretentious. It may be that the unpretentious Quakers gave Milton a hint as to how to represent a Christ-like human being, a living example of how to live purely and simply, while resisting evil successfully. Replies such as the "Mee worse then wet" show the Son as a dignified plain-speaker.

The subject of the patient Christ enduring temptation in the desert had often been celebrated in visual art and in brief epics such as the Roman Catholic and Vergilian short epic by Girolamo Vida, the four-book *Christiad* (1535), which concentrates more on the Passion than on the temptation of Christ. Milton, as one might expect, does not celebrate the iconography or sacred portraiture of Christ: his Son of Man is "obscure, / Unmark't, unknown" (1.24–5) when we first see him. His mother calls his life "Private, unactive, calm, contemplative, / Little suspicious to any King" (2.81–2). And, as in *Paradise Lost*, the focus of attention almost immediately becomes Satan, once again defined in terms of the meaning of his name, "the Adversary," who summons a demonic council as soon as he has overheard God proclaiming his "beloved Son" in the process of being baptized by John.

Before the epic's action begins, Milton's Son of God has distinguished himself in debates with the rabbis, as an early-blooming child of 12. When asked by his mother why he has spent so much time in precocious intellectual debate, his famous answer is "wist ye not that I must be about my father's business" (Luke 2:49), which is paraphrased by his mother in *Paradise Regain'd* at 2.99. For Milton, the debates with the rabbis equip the Son to go into combat with Satan fully prepared. Amongst the "doctors" so described in the Authorized Version, "all that heard him were astonished at his understanding and answers" (Luke 2:47).

The Satan of *Paradise Regain'd* is a diminished Satan from the beginning, as plainly marked as Cain, wounded and under sentence of death for what he has done to Adam and Eve and for the murder, "in ovo" or in the seed of humankind. The Son of God is the Seed destined to overcome Satan, ultimately.

As we have come to expect from his behavior in *Paradise Lost*, Satan lies from the beginning of the short epic, saying to his cohorts that John the Baptist only "Pretends to wash off sin" (1.73). When Satan tells the truth, he is a good reporter, noticing for instance that God's glory shines in his son's face, but we can sense that he is, from the start, a cosmic loser as well as a liar, with little to say of importance or consequence. He seems to have exhausted much of his creativity in being devious or even in lying. As the Son points out, "lying is [his] sustenance, [his] food" (1.429), so much a part of him that it becomes trite.

To give the devil his due, Satan is sometimes capable of the same simple eloquence that the Son practices, especially when he is reporting the truth, as when he describes the storms that might have frightened the average man but did not bother the Son as "harmless, if not wholsom, as a sneeze" (4.458).

His disguise as a simple shepherd or peasant type doesn't fool the Son very long at all. In disguise, he does not last as long as he had with Eve, who doesn't realize that the Serpent is Satan until after she and Adam fall. The Son sees through Satan's disguise even more quickly than the Lady detects Comus's false peasant pose.

Satan is no longer in any way a monarch as he was pictured monarch of Hell in the first book of *Paradise Lost*: he is merely "a great Dictator" (1.113), like an earthly emperor who has become a megalomaniac. Since being jeered or hissed at by his own troops of fallen angels, when he returns to address his legions after tempting Adam and Eve, he seems to realize that his time is over, that he is passé or out of step with the better sort of human beings, and that he can't win the battle with the eternal God or with the Son of God.

Epic devices and epithets

There are similes, catalogues, dream visions, flights "without wing /
Of *Hippocrif*" (4.541–2) through the middle and upper regions of air,
and demonic consults in the brief epic, but they all seem to be on a
smaller scale than the larger varieties of each epic device in *Paradise
Lost*. The Son at the beginning of Book 2 is "caught up to God, as
once / *Moses* was in the Mount, and missing long" (14–15). Such a
small simile as the comparison between the Son and Moses seems
truncated. Almost all the similes of the brief epic are just as brief:
Satan is compared with "one in City, or Court, or Palace bred" (2.100),
very simply, without ornamentation. By contrast, Satan's language
is usually ornate, metaphorical, colorful, but hollow and deceitful,
usually full of false comparisons, artificial coloring, and noise with
out much sense.

When Satan begins to tempt the Son in what is more or less his
own shape (you can never tell, with devils, what shape they may
assume), he looks very much like a courtier "Not rustic as before,
but seemlier clad" (2.300). Satan's seemly dress is, like his metaphors, unnecessarily ornamented, and his aristocratic pose is more
than suspicious: it is part of his living lie. But to associate Satan with
courtiers in 1671 is to satirize the court of Charles II, in power since
1660. The Restoration court was easily satirized for its luxury and
public immorality – its endorsement of what Milton would have
called the Sons of Belial, sponsors of drunkenness and debauchery.
The politics of *Paradise Regain'd* is populist and even democratic. The
simple carpenter who associated with fishermen rebukes the smooth
and hollow aristocratic poseur Satan.

As in *The Odyssey* and *The Iliad*, the author's moral position with
respect to characters can be found by examining epithets. If Odysseus
is "wily," then the poet encourages us to think of him as exemplifying wiliness. A search of the epithets for characters, or the adjectives
or adverbs the narrator uses to characterize them or their speech,
gives us a clue as to how Milton wants us to take them or value
them. At the same time, though, Milton associates formal poetic
epithets, or at least the Greek ones, with cheek-varnish. The Son
challenges the pagan Greek writers of "Fable, Hymn, or Song," to
"Remove their swelling Epithetes thick laid / As varnish on a Har-
lots cheek" (4.343–4). That challenge suggests that all ornamental

epithets are suspect, and it suggests that the rhetoric of *Paradise Regain'd* will be restrained, bare, and honest by comparison.

So it is. Here are the descriptive adjectives, adverbs, and epithets applied to Satan and the Son in Books 3 and 4:

Satan speaks	And the Son answers
At length collecting all his	calmly
Serpent wiles murmuring	fervently
struck / With the guilt of his	
own sin	
inly rackt	
new train of words began	
yet more presum'd	
	To whom our Saviour answer'd
	thus unmov'd
	to the Fiend / Made answer meet
Perplex'd and troubl'd at his bad	unmov'd
success	
impudent	with disdain
with fear abasht	sagely
Quite at a loss . . . with stern brow	meek and with untroubl'd mind
in a careless mood	in brief answer'd him
now swoln with rage	
in scorn	To whom thus Jesus
smitten with amazement	

This is a coldly selected catalogue of words carefully chosen to direct the reader's response toward loathing for Satan and respect for the Son. Satan must use Serpent wiles; he must murmur like a malcontent; he is inly racked with pain (as he was in Book 1 of *Paradise Lost*); he needs a train of words as compared with a simple progression; he presumes; he is perplexed and troubled; he feels fear and is; abashed and at a loss; he is frustratedly angry; he puts on a stern appearance and then the appearance of carelessness until he is found out, at which point he swells with rage and displays scorn but then falls, struck down by amazement at the power of God.

The Son reacts calmly, unbothered by Satan's moods, then he reacts fervently when righteous anger is called for; he does not need to pretend in his reactions; he is mild, meek (a word loaded with significance for Milton, because it indicates great self-control and patience in the midst of martyrdom); he answers sagely, with great wisdom; he is untroubled, dismissing Satan easily, briefly. He is centered, calm, unflustered, objective. He knows the battle is over without serious engagement.

Milton takes care to make the Son compare himself with the biblical Job and with the most famous martyr of the Greek world, Plato's martyr to freedom of thought, Socrates, mentioned by name twice in *Paradise Regain'd* (3.96; 4.274). The Son is like Job an isolated warrior against Satan in the desert. Socrates, having been executed by well-meaning men in Athens, serves as an historical parallel to the Son, who says he "For truths sake suffer[s] death unjust" (3.96). When Milton makes the Son compare himself to Socrates, the meaningful gesture validates the best of Greek thought and behavior. The Son supports the idea that Socrates' martyrdom for truth's sake during a tyrannical period in Athenian history is similar to what he will endure at the hands of Pontius Pilate. When the Son compares himself with Socrates, the reader has to think of the Greek philosopher, who died in 399 BCE, as a just man whose death prefigured that of Christ, and the Son allies Socrates with Job and then compares himself to the other two. All three men fight evil with personal integrity and courage, in the face of hardship, pain, and death.

In allying the Son with Socrates, Milton also seems to be foreshadowing and to some extent undercutting the Son's necessary rejection of pagan culture and pagan oracles – including most of the Greek system of religious belief – which will occur when the birth of Christ, as in Milton's Nativity Ode, silences the oracles of the pagan world. During the "Temptation of Athens" in Book 4, the Son will have to reject Satan's very reasonable and (for him) truthful presentation of Greek philosophy and art, in the cause of rejecting paganism – those sometimes worthy "shadowy types" of truth represented in Greek philosophy or Greek tragedy. Probably the reason that Milton saves that temptation for last is that it poses the strongest temptation for the author and for the reader. How could Milton the classicist, the tragedian, the epic writer, reject Plato, the Greek tragedians, and Homer himself? It hurts. And it has hurt generations of critics who find it difficult to reject classical culture in the name of Christianity.

The tension is palpable as Satan, as the tempter, gives a fair evaluation of Greek culture, speaking what seems to be Miltonic truth, and the Son must nevertheless reject that culture for the same reason that the infant Christ in Milton's Nativity Ode must silence the oracle of Apollo. From Milton's cultural perspective, paganism had to be replaced and superceded by Christianity.

Even as Milton has the Son denounce the "fabling" of Greek artists who were obliged to endorse a system of what he considered to be pagan gods, he still takes pain to set the Son within the historical context of the historical Jesus. The Emperor Tiberius, famous for his debauchery at Capri, is mentioned by the Son at 3.159, as Milton mixes what he knew about biblical history with what he learned from Roman historians such as Suetonius.

Satan is a courtier, well-dressed and smooth-talking, very much on the side of ostentatious wealth and gentility, in *Paradise Regain'd*. Again, Satan has taken his cue for dress and speech from Belial. On the other hand, like Socrates the Son is obscure, wilfully and intentionally poor, a working-class carpenter (2.414) as Socrates was a sculptor. The Son is to Satan as Samson is to Harapha in *Samson Agonistes*, a peasant or day-laborer facing someone of exalted social position and rank. Milton presents him as a member of the sympathetic, plain-speaking underclass, as if God were to reveal himself on that level of society rather than in palaces. Milton was not a Leveler by theological profession – he does not wish to put all social activity or human relations on the equal level of Adam and Eve before the Fall – but he held no value in useless or ostentatious or hollow aristocracy.

The brief epic never really strays far from the personal or the domestic sphere. The Son of God has a mother and a home, and, in a remarkably quiet ending (as with Adam and Eve holding hands at the end of *Paradise Lost* or with the survivors in *Samson Agonistes* reflecting on "all passion spent"), the Son, having defeated the author of all evil, simply returns home to his mother's house. His mother's house is what gives meaning to his human life: he is centered there. And Mary, the mother of this Son, is herself the opposite of the idolized Virgin Mary: she is simple, plain-speaking, sweet, gentle, modest, and loving. She is a dear mother, not an amplified icon. Milton significantly gives her more of a speaking part than she has in the Bible, but she remains a mother, not a symbol.

We know that the Son will face the crucifixion at the end of his life, but Milton's short epic is concerned with events toward the beginning of the Son's adult or professional career, and it dwells on his positive and definitive victory over Satan, rather than on his tortured death.

As one might expect from the scope of a brief epic, all art or artfulness is scaled down or even miniaturized, including the similes and metaphors. And the lack of pretentiousness or religiosity in Milton's picture of the Son's human family carries over into the Son's language and the Son's speaking style, which is abrupt, curt with Satan, and in general the opposite of courtly or ornamented. Because he speaks mostly to Satan, the Son is allowed sarcasm and angry phrases: his is righteous indignation, very much like the Lady's when she calls Comus "fool" or "juggler." It is part of Milton's constantly enforced decorum to allow his righteous figures to insult the Devil, or belittle him. This is war, after all, between good and evil. Evil should be treated with cold scorn.

Samson Agonistes

Critics and biographers have argued for over fifty years whether *Samson Agonistes* is an early work – outlined in the 1640s, perhaps – or a work composed after Milton had himself been put in the position of Samson because of the Restoration of Charles II (1660). In 1649, as the champion of Parliament after the execution of Charles I, Milton had taken an active part in breaking the image of King Charles I as a martyr in *Eikonoklastes*. But in 1660 Milton was a member of an alien party, a labeled regicide, an enemy of the new state; he was blind and therefore defenseless; he may have felt himself to be a kind of strongman buffoon, laughed at and scorned by the new courtiers in power; and he had little hope of vengeance on his political oppressors. It is very tempting to say that *Samson Agonistes* represents his wish fulfillment for a righteous victory over his own oppressors. Milton would not be the only parliamentarian or Cromwellian who after 1660 fancied the role of David as giant-killer or of Samson, the righteous avenger.

The title page of the little volume that houses both *Paradise Regain'd* and *Samson Agonistes* tantalizes with its vagueness, since the dramatic poem is described as a tag-along: it is the epic first, "to which is added Samson Agonistes." Close examinations of the stylistics of

Samson Agonistes reveal that it is a very late work in Milton's poetic career, much closer to *Paradise Regain'd* in its poetic economy than to the Nativity Ode. When the Chorus makes the oracular pronouncement "Just are the ways of God, / And justifiable to Men" (293–4), Milton certainly seems to be alluding to and echoing the opening of *Paradise Lost*, where the narrator claims to "assert Eternal Providence / And justifie the wayes of God to men" (1.25–6). And Milton's feisty defense of unrhymed heroic poetry, despite his own constant use of rhymes in *Samson Agonistes*, points to his own Restoration conflict between writing in the blank verse of *Paradise Lost* and following the fashion of poets like Andrew Marvell and John Dryden, who always wrote rhymed poetry, usually in heroic couplets. Milton is working against fashion and poetic custom: a rebellious Samson deserves a verse form that defies current custom; the play is not a tragedy exactly, but a dramatic poem.

Milton has it every which way. He will not allow his Royalist reader the satisfaction of performing his play because it is not a play, and he will not give in to the fashion to write about heroes using only heroic couplets. If he uses rhyme, he will hide it, and not display it regularly every other line.

Milton will not allow his reader to take any element of his dramatic poem on face value. As his preface, "*Of that sort of Dramatic Poem which is call'd Tragedy*," announces, the dramatic poem will have all the elements of Greek tragedy, but each of those elements will be transmuted, reshaped using a kind of revolutionary poetics. A potentially barbaric and heathen revenge myth will be rewritten from a Christian perspective, yet the play will retain most of the elements of Greek tragedy – the chorus working in choral odes, the struggle, the hero with the tragic flaw identified by the term hubris, the messenger to report on violence occurring offstage.

The very tension between Hebraic folk-tale elements in the story (a riddling trickster hero, yet a judge) and Christian redemption has set critics abuzz since the earliest readers responded to what Milton wrote. Samson's story in Judges is that of a larger than lifesize gloryhog and buffoon, a trickster tricked, a fool used by the God of Israel to exact vengeance on the Philistines for keeping the tribes of Israel in bondage. On the face of it, Samson is a mass-murderer and a suicide, but his pulling down the temple does seem to fulfill some sort of pattern of godly vengeance, and it does provoke a kind of catharsis, as in "Thank God that's over" – a natural reaction to a catastrophe when a temple is collapsed onto hundreds of people.

A woman has given a man a haircut. That should not be so significant, but when the biblical Delilah cuts Samson's hair the act is symbolic – almost Freudian, in that she has learned that the secret of his masculine strength lies in the length of his hair, and she has decided to betray him as an Israelite of the tribe of Dan to her people, the Philistines, by cutting it off. Milton's imagery reinforces the association of emasculation and defeat. According to Milton's Samson, she makes him into a "tame wether," a meek castrated ram, when she cuts off his – hair. The images of hair-cutting and castration are deliberately mixed. Samson is even upset with God, at first, because the secret of his Nazarite's strength is hung in his hair, something so fragile and apparently meaningless

Milton's Samson, unlike the biblical Samson who pays Delilah as a prostitute, has married his Dalila. Milton insists on that spelling, possibly because it fits his iambic line more comfortably, being accented on the first and third syllables. Dalila is not just a Philistine and a worshiper of the false god Dagon, she is a "bosom snake": she betrays the sacred bond of matrimony, putting her degenerate tribe and her idol-worshiping religion before her domestic loyalty to her husband. First appearances do count: when she enters the scene, she looks like a prostitute or a gaudy ship under full sail; she even smells seductive to her alienated husband; her words are unctuous and she sounds a great deal like Milton's Satan at his most seductive with Eve. Samson as seen by the audience is quietly powerful and sexy; Dalila is noisy, colorful, and perfumed. The love she offers Samson is soft, luxurious, enervating, too easy: she will be his seductive caretaker in his blindness. He must resist the impulse to be cared for, since to give in to that would be weak and, in seventeenth-century terminology, "effeminate."

Dalila has seduced a few critics into thinking that she is an empowered woman and therefore liberated or free-thinking, but it is hard to think of her in any other but evil terms. She has emasculated her husband, she has betrayed him to hypocritical priests, and she has sold him into slavery. She wants only her own glory, and, if she became his caretaker, she would reduce him to something like a luxurious vegetative state. Samson would become Dalila's boy toy or couch potato – a horrible existence for a former war hero. Among the Dagon-worshipers, Dalila is a hero, an emancipator of her tribe, but, to Israel, she has betrayed their champion and their judge.

The tragic hero, according to Milton following Aristotle, was supposed to undergo the equivalent of a wrestling match, his agon, or in this case his deadly struggle. Milton makes the struggle of his tragic hero internal. Samson struggles with his own conscience, with his responsibilities towards his family, with his relationship to his wife-betrayer, with his burden as judge of the Israelites and with his role as their deliverer. He must consider his slave duty to the Philistian lords as his duty, a noble service not to the Philistines but to the tribes of Israel, to carry out God's purpose as embodied in his life as a Nazarite, one chosen of God for divine purposes on earth.

As Barbara Lewalski points out (526–33), the dramatic poem is organized in a series of agons. Samson must resist the blandishments of Dalila, on his own, as she claims to want to take him home and cuddle him. He has to ignore or shrug off the taunts of Harapha, as compared with his feral desire to tear the giant apart. He has to suffer ulcerously with the guilt laid on him by the Chorus and by his father Manoa, for marrying infidel women, women who are not of his faith or citizenship, recklessly. He also must wrestle with his own past errors, vanities, and proud but foolish acts, such as setting grain fields on fire by sending in foxes with blazing tails.

Milton's Samson is more than the sum of the biblical muscleman's parts: he has a psychological and spiritual depth impossible to find in the Samson story in Judges without a wealth of biblical commentary on the story to aid a reader. Samson is to begin with at the end of his rope, a ragged, dirty, thoughtful old strong man, and his divine purpose in life, embodied in his long hair and Nazarite faith, seems to have been blunted by his having had his hair cut by Dalila, by his having been blinded, and by his having been reduced to slavery and side-show performances of strength for the worshipers of Dagon. He can sink no lower than he has at the beginning of the play, and he refers to himself as a being without hope, in despair, in the depths of depression. He is an unlikely judge and prophet, or hero, saint, or savior. But, through his successful struggle with his own demons, and through divine inspiration or "divine motions" in him, he comes back to life and becomes a deliverer of the Israelites, and a martyr.

Unlike the tragic hero Hamlet, Samson doesn't have to escape from pirates, jump in graves, test the veracity of a ghost, or fight a duel. Unlike Oedipus, he does not put out his own eyes, nor does his mother or wife commit suicide, as does Jocasta. Samson's actions are all internalized. He is a tragic hero with an ulcerated soul, fighting off despair. He is not an action hero.

Samson Agonistes is more like a radio play, a drama heard in the head, a tragedy as performed in the mind of a blind man, than it is like a stage play. It is perhaps made more powerful by being heard rather than seen, because it occupies the mind through the sound of its dialogue. It is a dramatic poem written by a blind man for an audience with its eyes closed. Uniquely, it might work on the stage if powerful actors recited their lines in total darkness – the dark amidst the blaze of noon that Samson alludes to – while the audience listened to the magnificent declamatory speeches of the play. The speeches demand complete concentration from any actor reading them and from any audience listening to them. They are anything but naturalistic, when one compares them to the quick dialogue of a mature Shakespearean tragedy or comedy: by comparison, the speeches in *Samson Agonistes* play more like a series of soliloquys.

Action does happen in the play, even violent action, but it is described in the manner of Greek tragedy, offstage. Milton has the best of a number of genres, and he knows what he is doing, combining various modes of poetry without the rigid formalism of Greek tragedy's choric strophes and counterstrophes. Milton builds the choric turns and counterturns and stands into choral speeches, but he does not call attention to the classical vestiges left in his dramatic structure. A chorus may be answered by a semi-chorus at times (1660–1707), so that the reader can respond to the illusion, at least, of a dialogue between members of the chorus, and there are even times when the Chorus speaks in verse paragraphs (1010–61), as if talking to itself in different voices, but without the division into chorus and semi-chorus.

Samson Agonistes requires of its audience the attention of the reader of lyric poetry, the imagination of the fiction reader, and the objectivity of the audience of tragic theater, ancient and modern, open to interpretations by actors and directors. As usual when he plays creatively with genre, Milton has it several ways at the same time. *Samson Agonistes* is a play that isn't a play; it is a Greek tragedy which uses elements of Shakespearean tragedy, in blank verse that might be

derived partly from Shakespearean usage but is also operatic in an
Italian modern style of declamatory tragedy. Handel would write
music for the tragedy 100 years after Milton wrote it, treating it as a
dramatic oratorio. Milton increases the range of tragedy as he writes
what has been called the last of the great Elizabethan tragedies, and
he may be mocking future generations of readers for thinking that
Samson Agonistes is only a play.

The middle of Milton's tragedy is taken up with Dalila and with
Harapha, a kind of fee-fie-foe-fum giant who is kin to Goliath and
thus associated with Goliath's defeat by the boy David. Blind and in
chains, Samson should be no match for Harapha, but Harapha is a
coward, an effete aristocratic athlete without brains, who runs from
Samson because Samson, he says, is dirty and needs a bath.

The Harapha episode is the comic relief of *Samson Agonistes*: the
big, dumb oaf is defeated hands down by the ever-nobler Samson,
secure in his spiritual strength. As a political figure, Harapha stands
for the confederacy of aristocrats, priests or prelates, and cavalier
military that the political Milton always fought against. The Dagonite
priests who whisper in Dalila's ear and provide her with money are
very like Laudian prelates as Milton imagined them in the 1640s.

By now it should be obvious: Milton imprints on Samson his own
fears as a helpless blind man who remembers what it was like to
have his sight. Bitterly, Samson inveighs against being taken care of
by well-meaning or proprietary custodians appointed for his wel-
fare. His father Manoa would have loved to have taken his son out
of the line of fire and ransomed him from the Philistines, buying his
son's freedom to come home. But Samson does have a mission and
a duty to purge Israel of Philistine rule; he has a civic duty as one
who has memories of being a judge; and he has a military duty to
exact vengeance on the enemies of his people, by catastrophically
destroying them and himself in the ruin of their temple. He can't go
home again.

And the lap of Dalila, where he had had his strength cut off with
his hair, is a treacherous, enervating, dangerous place to be, no matter
how tempting it is to be fondled and cuddled by an attractive and
sensuous woman.

Ambiguities of the tragedy

The Chorus of Israelites in Milton's tragedy doesn't always say the right thing. They can be as misguided as a chorus in a play by Euripides, and they may make the wrong judgment for the wrong reasons. At times they seem one cut above a mob, and at times they seem to speak what seems to be the Miltonic version of the truth. At times it is very hard for a modern reader to know which is which, especially when the chorus talks about marriages gone wrong, when a bride who looks "Soft, modest, meek, demure" turns out to be "A cleaving mischief" who "by her charms / Draws him awry enslav'd / With dotage, and his sense deprav'd / To folly and shameful deeds which ruin ends" (1039 45). The chorus may be describing Samson's marriage, but there is always a chance that the description may be universal and that the chorus is projecting an image of most marriages.

Also, when the crestfallen Harapha leaves in cowardly retreat, the chorus comments, "Oh how comely it is and how reviving / To the Spirits of just men long opprest! / When God into the hands of thir deliverer / Puts invincible might / To quell the mighty of the Earth" (1268–72). At that point the chorus seems to celebrate Samson's bloodthirsty defeat of Philistine giants. Then the Chorus turns to discuss the better fortitude of "plain Heroic magnitude of mind / And celestial vigour" (1280–1), which seems to be a less controversial position. The reader who remembers *Paradise Lost* and its "violent Lords" such as the mighty hunter Nimrod (12.80) associates violence with tyranny and with the narrator's comment "Tyrannie must be / Though to the Tyrant thereby no excuse" (12.95–6).

There are times when the Chorus seems level-headed and Miltonic and there are times when they endorse behavior we know Milton would not approve of – as when they commend Manoa for wanting to ransom his son rather than allowing him to fulfill his fate. Perhaps the ambiguity of the Chorus, and indeed the plot of the tragedy of Samson, a warrior hero humiliated by his Philistine enemies, who wreaks a horrible vengeance on the Philistines in suicidal violence, expresses Milton himself poised between two wrongs at the Restoration and wanting mercy for himself at the same time as wanting vengeance on his enemies. Milton's isolation, his political defeat, his anger with what he considered to be the unjust restoration of an illegitimate monarchy together with its priestly system, his desire for vengeance that his theology would not normally allow a Christian to exact – all of those ambiguous and frustrating tensions are built into the plot and character of Samson and his adversaries. The very dating of the poem, establishing that it was surely written after the Restoration, has been very important to the critics of the last 50 years, because it is so important to the understanding of the tragedy to see Milton's isolation as its major motivating force. A blind, strong, betrayed, heroic, depressed, slavish old man is what Milton was, and what Samson is.

The dust has settled on the temple of Dagon at the end of *Samson Agonistes*, and a kind of peace settles over vindicated Israel, whose enemies have been killed by their hero, catastrophically. Milton returns to the rules of Aristotle that he outlines very cleverly in his preface to *Samson Agonistes*, especially to the power of tragedy "by raising pity and fear, or terror, to purge the mind of those and such like passion, that is to temper and reduce them to just measure with a kind of delight" (*Riverside* 799). Milton's tragedy ends with "all passion spent," its catastrophe purging pity and fear from the mind of its reader (even if Milton denies his reader the possibility of seeing a tragedy not intended for the stage, as he tells us it was not [800]).

Aftermath and Influence

"One's country is where it is well with one" – Milton wrote those revealing words in a Latin letter written in 1666, to a friend from Cleves, Peter Heimbach. In his early optimistic years, when he could picture his country as a kind of eagle arising from sleep into ferocity and pride, Milton was chauvinistic toward England, proud to celebrate its heroes and its history. He was also a kind of citizen of the world, that rare Englishman whose independent wealth allowed him to see what he considered to be the civilized world, western Europe from France to southern Italy (he wanted to visit Greece as the cradle of western civilization, and he might have visited the Holy Land, but changes in plans did not permit either journey). His mastery of the universal language Latin allowed him to speak to educated people everywhere, and his knowledge of romance languages made him very comfortable in Italy, though perhaps a little less so in France.

By the end of his life, with the defeat of his own political cause, with blindness, in fear of execution or assassination, with occasional but serious family turmoil, Milton became what Louis Martz has sensitively labeled a "poet of exile." His *Paradise Lost* is pervaded by a sense of loss, a sense of isolation, a sense of homelessness. It "ultimately denies all loyalties to any institution of the state" (Corns 142). Of course to say that is not to imply suicidal despair or hopelessness. The fact that Milton could write such a wonderful poem affirms the life in it, despite the fact that Milton pictures the loss of paradise and the exile of Adam and Eve.

Milton's reputation has always bristled with controversy, mostly because he was a republican and a regicide at the Restoration. He was a king-killing poet, embraced for all the wrong reasons by the Whig party as a parliamentarian or libertarian, and occasionally embraced by Tories as the greatest English epic poet, someone who, like Shakespeare, stands for the best that England can do. Every word of Samuel Johnson's great biography of Milton is edgy with hatred for what Milton stood for: he was a "vile Whig" to Johnson.

Paradise Lost and Milton were welcomed to the canon of great English poetry when, in 1688, a group of conservative Oxfordians centered at Christ Church produced a folio edition of Milton's poem, putting him in that small group of English poets, such as Ben Jonson, William Shakespeare, or Michael Drayton, to deserve such an enormous book brought forth in their honor. The volume was sold by subscription, payment in advance in return for a name listed amongst the subscribers, and it was prefaced by a handsome portrait with a short poem by John Dryden declaring that Milton was in a direct line from Homer and Vergil. Dryden had already tried his hand at reducing Milton's epic to his own puppet operetta in couplets, *The State of Innocence*, which had been entered in the Stationers' Register as if in competition with the second edition of *Paradise Lost*, in 1674. Dryden was purported to have said "This man cuts us all out," in the spirit of competitive poetasting. The 1674 edition of *Paradise Lost* seems to be making fun of the "tinkling rhymes" of Dryden's couplets in Milton's word to the reader, and Andrew Marvell alludes to Dryden's verse in terms of tired packhorses and putting tags on things that don't need tags. Even Milton's very first imitator, in other words, must have felt what Harold Bloom has brilliantly labeled the anxiety of influence.

By 1712 or so Milton's epic, at least, was thought to be a classic, and Joseph Addison could devote an issue a week of the *Spectator*, for months, producing the first book-length study of Milton's work, but in the very popular medium of an early news journal. Addison, a political moderate, could forget about Milton as king-killer and concentrate on his work as sublime poetry.Even after death, Milton proved a formidable competitor with the poets who emulated him in the eighteenth century, during which the consummate form of poetry was thought to be the epic, but during which no great epic, or even heroic tragedy, was produced. Nicholas von Maltzahn has been busy lately tracing the influence of "the Miltonic sublime" on aesthetic theorists of the eighteenth century. Even John Phillips, Milton's nephew and pupil, was to try his hand at making money by imitating his uncle's poetry blatantly, lifting whole phrases from *Paradise Lost*, a poem possibly dictated, in part, to John Phillips, who may have served as his uncle's amanuensis from time to time. This John Phillips (there was another poet by that name) broke from his uncle's politics but still capitalized on his uncle's growing reputation.

Those critics or poets who could put aside Milton's politics (not to mention his social or educational or domestic agendas) could appreciate what Christopher Ricks would call "Milton's Grand Style" and which some nineteenth-century critics might sentimentalize as "Milton's organ voice." In Samuel Johnson's mid-century biography and criticism, however, there is only grudging praise for Milton as a national landmark. Johnson obviously hated the man and only half-heartedly endorsed the poetry, making cutting remarks such as the famous comment on *Paradise Lost* that no one ever wished it longer than it is. As a journalist, Johnson was all but obsessed with finding any rumor on record that might blacken Milton's character, such as his being read to by his daughters in languages they could not understand, and painting that rumor as a distinguishing mark of Milton's personality, until Johnson could make outrageous comments as when he wrote that Milton had "a Turkish contempt for women" – a blatantly false statement, but one that keeps surfacing in Milton criticism, like a bad penny.

Johnson, however, profoundly respected Milton's learning and, after all is said and done, his poetry as well. Milton is cited as often as any English poet in Johnson's *Dictionary*, produced in the 1750s, and he is cited with respect for his command of English usage, and his originality, along with his profound sense of the etymology of any English word he used. Johnson also had to respect Milton's learning and his linguistic ability, though at times Johnson made fun of displays of learning in poems like "Lycidas."

Poets from Pope to Blake, Wordsworth, and Shelley had to know Milton well. Milton shows up as an ambiguously inspirational figure, his Serpent made into a potential liberating force, in Blake's *Milton*, and Milton's Satan and his Promethean creature Adam both are ever-present in Mary Shelley's *Frankenstein*. Any given Baron Frankenstein or any given Monster in any number of horror movies based on the great book is apt at least to quote Mary Shelley quoting Milton. In popular culture, Milton's Satan as well as generic Adams and Eves keep returning, especially in the cinema. Robert De Niro and Mickey Rourke have both played Satan figures, and Al Pacino recently played a Satanic lawyer named "John Milton," in the film *The Devil's Advocate*. There is even a Mike Figgis film, *The Loss of Sexual Innocence* (2000), which contrasts modern-day gender politics and sexual manipulation with the innocence and fall of a naked Adam and Eve.

It is difficult to stage any version of a dramatized *Paradise Lost*, though the Polish-American composer Krzysztof Penderecki composed the music for a *sacra rappresentazione* (something like a dramatic oratorio, with limited movement on state, based on a sacred text), its libretto by Christopher Fry, first produced at the Chicago Lyric Opera in 1978. The opera attempts to set to music Adam and Eve's long speeches as recitatives and arias, for a performance in two acts. Adam and Eve, incidentally, were in body stockings and not nude, and the angel Zephon had a part, as did Beelzebub and Death.

In modern dance, the brilliant Mark Morris has with great commercial success choreographed his New York-based troupe to perform to Handel's setting of *L'Allegro, Il Penseroso, and Il Moderato*. Suzanne Weiss reviewed a performance at Berkeley, in California, in May, 2000:

> There is a verse in Milton's L'Allegro that may have inspired Morris to craft this highly innovative dance: "Come, and trip it as you go, on

the light fantastic toe." His dancers can trip the light fantastic with the best of them, as was amply proved in the opening of this week's engagement at Zellerbach Hall in Berkeley. Framed by a system of colorful sliding panels and screens that subtly change the configuration of the stage from scene to scene, they leap and twirl, somersault and crawl on all fours. They prance like horses and climb upon each other's backs, forming human pyramids that gracefully unravel again.

Sometimes the movement mirrors the words (which are not always audibly intelligible, in spite of the careful articulation of the singers). If the verse speaks of sight, the dancers cover their eyes. If someone sings of rivers and streams, dancers lie down and undulate like the waves. An ode to the lark and the nightingale has a soloist fluttering his arms like wings.

A fine 1992 recording of Handel's setting of the twin poems and *Il Moderato*, a much inferior but classically proportioned middle section, exists, with John Eliot Gardiner conducting the English Baroque Soloists (Wea/Atlantic/Erato – #45377).

Works Cited

Achinstein, Sharon. *Milton and the Revolutionary Reader*. Princeton, NJ: Princeton University Press, 1994.

Beal, Peter. *In Praise of Scribes: Manuscripts and their Makers in Seventeenth-Century England*. Oxford: Clarendon Press, 1998.

Blakiston, Noel. "Milton's Birthplace." *London Topographical Record*, 19 (1947): 6–12.

Breasted, Barbara. "Another Bewitching of Lady Alice Egerton, the Lady of *Comus*." *Notes & Queries*, NS 17 (or 215) (1970): 411–12.

Brown, Cedric. *John Milton's Aristocratic Entertainments*. Cambridge: Cambridge University Press, 1985.

Buehler, Stephen. "'How Charming is Divine Philosophy!': Music, Magic, and Thought in Milton's Masque." Newberry Library Milton Seminar on Medieval and Early Modern Magic. 11 May 2001 [not yet published].

Campbell, Gordon. *A Milton Chronology*. London: Macmillan Press, 1997.

—— "Shakespeare and the Youth of Milton." *Milton Quarterly*, 33 (1999): 95–105.

Columbia see Milton, John, *The Works*.

Corns, Thomas. "Milton and the Characteristics of a Free Commonwealth." In Himy and Skinner, *Milton and Republicanism*, 25–42.

—— *Regaining* Paradise Lost. London: Longman, 1994.

—— *Uncloistered Virtue: English Political Literature, 1640–1660*. Oxford: Clarendon Press, 1992.

Danielson, Dennis. *Milton's Good God: A Study of Literary Theodicy*. Cambridge: Cambridge University Press, 1982.

Darbishire, Helen (ed.). *The Early Lives of Milton*. New York: Barnes & Noble, 1965.

Ellwood, Thomas. *The History of the Life of Thomas Ellwood, Written by his own hand*, ed. S. Graveson. London: Headley Brothers, 1906.

Empson, William. *Milton's God*. Rev. edn. London: Chatto & Windus, 1965.

Evans, J. Martin. "The Birth of the Author: Milton's Poetic Self-Construction." *Milton Studies*, 38 (2000): 47–65.

French, J. Milton. *Life Records of John Milton*. 5 vols. New Brunswick, NJ: Rutgers University Press, 1950–8; reprint, Gordion, 1966.

Helgerson, Richard. *Self-Crowned Laureates: Spenser, Jonson, Milton and the Literary System*. Berkeley and Los Angeles: University of California Press, 1983.

Himy, Armand, and Skinner, Quentin (eds.). *Milton and Republicanism*. Cambridge: Cambridge University Press, 1995.

Hunter, William B., Jr. *Milton's* Comus: *Family Piece*. Troy, NY: Whitston Publishing Company, 1983.

Illo, John. "*Areopagitica*s Mythic and Real." *Prose Studies*, 11 (1988): 3–23.

Johnson, Samuel. *Selected Poetry and Prose*, ed. Frank Brady and W. K. Wimsatt. Berkeley: University of California Press, 1977.

Lewalski, Barbara. *The Life of John Milton: A Critical Biography*. Oxford: Blackwell, 2000.

McGuire, Maryann Cale. *Milton's Puritan Masque*. Athens: University of Georgia Press, 1983.

Marvell, Andrew. *The Poems and Letters of Andrew Marvell*, ed. H. M. Margoliouth. 3rd edn. Oxford: Clarendon Press, 1971.

Martz, Louis L. *Poet of Exile: A Study of Milton's Poetry*. New Haven: Yale University Press, 1980.

Milton, John. *The Complete Prose Works*, gen. ed. Don M. Wolfe. 8 vols. New Haven: Yale University Press, 1953–82.

—— *The Riverside Milton*, ed. Roy Flannagan. Boston: Houghton Mifflin, 1998.

—— *The Works of John Milton*, gen. ed. Frank A. Patterson. 20 vols. New York: Columbia University Press, 1931–8.

Parker, William Riley. *Milton: A Biography*. 2nd edn., ed. Gordon Campbell. Oxford: Clarendon Press, 1996.

Riverside see Milton, John, *The Riverside Milton*.

Shawcross, John T. *John Milton: The Self and the World*. Lexington: University Press of Kentucky, 1993.

Stow, John. *The Survey of London*, ed. H. B. Wheatley. London: Dent, 1987.

Wittreich, Joseph. "'Reading' Milton: The Death (and Survival) of the Author." *Milton Studies*, 38 (2000): 10–46.

Yale see Milton, John, *Complete Prose Works*.

Zivley, Sherry Lutz. "The Thirty-Three Days of *Paradise Lost*." *Milton Quarterly*, 34 (2000): 117–27.

Index